FLIRT FEARLESSLY

ADVANCED PRAISE

"Happiness is the ultimate quest in life. *Flirt Fearlessly* shows you how to be happy while dating, no mater what the situation. Anyone who is single (or who wants a closer relationship with their spouse) needs to read this book!"

Elizabeth Lombardo, Ph.D., author of the bestselling book, *A Happy You: Your Ultimate Prescription for Happiness*

"Flirting is supposed to be fun, but frankly, it can be intimidating! Rachel DeAlto has the solution for anyone who's ever needed the boost of confidence to get what they want. Certainly a must have in a single's dating tool kit!"

Maria Avgitidis, Matchmaker & Dating Coach, Agape Match

"Flirting can be safe AND sexy… frisky AND fun, if you do it like Rachel DeAlto! Carrie Bradshaw & Co. could have saved themselves a lot of effort if they'd had this helpful handbook when they were running around NYC. Guys might learn a few useful tricks in these pages, too!"

Nelson Aspen, International Entertainment Journalist & Author, *Hollywood Insider: Exposed!*

"Rachel's lighthearted and fun book can make even the most fearful of flirters jump in with confidence. This is a must-read for everyone who wants to "get their flirt on!"

Bela Gandhi, Founder, Smart Dating Academy

"If you have ever wondered 'What if?' about someone you thought was cute, but didn't have the guts to approach—this book is for you."

Julie Spira, CEO, bestselling author, online dating expert and CEO Cyber-Dating Expert

"Falling in love is the easy part. Communicating our interest to a potential target of our affection on the other hand can reduce the most confident romantic into a stammering mess. Rachel's book on flirting fearlessly can help the tongue-tied and fearful find love and--most importantly--enjoy the process of getting there."

Harrison Monarth, New York Times bestselling author of *The Confident Speaker*

FLIRT FEARLESSLY

The A to Z Guide to Getting Your Flirt On

Rachel DeAlto

NEW YORK

Flirt Fearlessly

The A to Z Guide to Getting Your Flirt On

ISBN 978-1-61448-374-8 paperback
ISBN 978-1-61448-375-5 eBook
Library of Congress Control Number: 2012947604

Morgan James Publishing
The Entrepreneurial Publisher
5 Penn Plaza, 23rd Floor, New York City, New York 10001
(212) 655-5470 office • (516) 908-4496 fax
www.MorganJamesPublishing.com

In an effort to support local communities, raise awareness and funds, Morgan James Publishing donates a percentage of all book sales for the life of each book to Habitat for Humanity Peninsula and Greater Williamsburg.

Get involved today, visit
www.MorganJamesBuilds.com.

For amazing singles everywhere who might need that little extra push to go after what (or who) they want. Give it a shot—you might be surprised with the results!

CONTENTS

Preface   *x*

Introduction   *xiii*

CHAPTER ONE
Ready. Set. Go!   **19**

CHAPTER TWO
Where to Get Your Flirt On   **35**

CHAPTER THREE
Your Right-Hand Wingman (or Wingwoman)   **57**

CHAPTER FOUR
Safety First   **67**

CHAPTER FIVE
5 Steps to Super Flirt   **83**

CHAPTER SIX
Breaking the Ice   **113**

CHAPTER SEVEN
Moving Your Body   **123**

CHAPTER EIGHT
That's Why They Make Strawberry and Mint Chocolate Chip   **133**

CHAPTER NINE
What the Heck Do I Do Now?   **145**

CHAPTER TEN
The Digital Flirt   **161**

CHAPTER ELEVEN
Taking Over the World   **177**

CHAPTER TWELVE
The Quiz   **183**

Conclusion   *189*

About the Author   *191*

PREFACE

You may be wondering who I am and how I got to the point that I felt compelled to write a book about flirting. Well, I am a flirt. An unabashed, unapologetic, shameless flirt. I have been a flirt since I was a child. Never afraid to talk with strangers (my parents had a slight issue with that…), always ready to give a compliment to perk someone up, and always wanting to make connections. It didn't always work, of course … it took years to learn how to flirt effectively and read the signals when my flirting wasn't appreciated. My earliest "romantic" flirtations (that I can remember) started when I was 5 or 6 years old. I had a streak of love letter writing in grammar school, but sadly, it just didn't take. I'd like to blame it on the recipient's lack of appreciation for my prose, but it was probably more likely due to bad perms, baby weight, and the fact that I was somewhat of a book nerd. It didn't exactly fuel my confidence during those years, but I eventually grew into my own (and grew out that hair). High school was fun, college was a blast, and by the time I reached my 20's I started to have an idea of who I was (and I liked her!). When you mix an ability to flirt with confidence, it is a magical combination. By the time I hit my 30s, I was unstoppable. I am very blessed in my love life.

So how does someone become a flirting expert? I wasn't always in this line of work, but it has become a passion and I cannot imagine ever doing anything else. It's a whole lot different than working as a civil trial attorney, that's for sure. When I was a practicing lawyer, no one was asking me about pick-up lines or the "right amount" of chest hair. I was always flirting, though—platonically—with the jury, with the judges, my co-workers—everyone. I have always used flirtation to my advantage to connect with people to help achieve an intended result. I'll never forget my first trial. It was a hysterical case that involved feather boas and firemen, but I vividly remember engaging with the jury to the point that when a witness got hostile with me, the jury members got pissed—they wanted to protect me! It was amazing and I realized just how powerful it is to connect with people on a human level— whether you want to date them, befriend them, work for them, or have them work for you. Engaging with people in a genuine and charismatic way has done me well. Trust me—there was a lot of learning from my mistakes! I have had some horrible dating experiences, some amazing relationships, and have gotten myself into situations where my flirtations were taken the "wrong way" (like when opposing counsel in the aforementioned trial asked me out to celebrate my winning of the case—even though winning the case, meant that he lost! I am here to share my "research" with you, dear reader! I want to help you avoid the pitfalls I have encountered, and use the techniques that have worked for me so you can have as much fun flirting and dating as I have had.

The truth is that I have been learning and growing since the first grade, and taking mental notes of what worked and what didn't work. I have also always played confidant and counselor for my friends. I have enjoyed and been humbled by their level of trust in me to help them in all areas of their love lives—from playing wingwoman, to the 3 a.m. phone calls when someone had broken their heart. The advice in the following pages is been inspired by issues that have come up for my clients, my friends, and myself. My years in the dating industry have shown me that these issues are commonplace among all singles, and my hope is that this book can help you to avoid those mistakes, and get your flirt on with confidence!

INTRODUCTION

My grandmother always told me that you catch more flies with honey. I was never really into bugs so the real meaning of what she was telling me didn't sink in until I got a little older. Of course, I eventually realized she was saying that being kind, complimentary and genuine was going to win people over a hell of a lot faster than being ornery and whiney. She might not have been telling me to go out and flirt (which would have been really odd), but she was telling me to put on a smile and be warm and inviting. Ultimately, I don't see much of a difference between being warm, genuine, and complimentary and *flirting*—which is why this book is here: to redefine the flirt, and to empower people to put their fears aside, and get their flirt on!

What is flirting? Is it always about seduction? Is it ever inappropriate to flirt? Am I going to look desperate or "easy" if I flirt? No! Flirting isn't anything to be ashamed of—flirting is something to be embraced! Flirting is a form of communication—a communication that allows you to make others feel good, make yourself feel good, and achieve a desired result. And that desired result is not always a date. Sometimes you will flirt completely platonically, often with friends or even business colleagues. Flirting can be used in every situation to bring a little more positivity into your life and the lives of others. Flirting is an art form and when it's done right, it will never, ever, feel dirty or wrong.

I like to think of FLIRT this way:

- F—Making people FEEL good
- L—LISTENING to others
- I—Making a positive IMPACT
- R—RADIATING warmth
- T—TAKING chances

As you can see, I believe the FLIRT as defined does not stand for anything related to sex. Of course, there are many people who believe that flirtation is synonymous with sexual seduction. While it can definitely be used for that, its potential usefulness is actually far broader. Flirtation is a tool, and like any very useful tool, it has a multitude of applications.

What situations can we flirt in? Flirting is truly about bringing positivity to yourself and others, and it can be used in nearly any situation. You may not realize it, and you may not have ever thought about it, but people flirt in business, in platonic relationships, and in almost every situation in which people are thrown together.

However, I am pretty sure that you bought this book to focus on the more seductive form of flirting, which I am all about as well. Flirting romantically hasn't changed a whole lot from the prehistoric days through the 21st century—minus the man throwing the woman over his shoulder and taking her back to the cave to mate. Much of flirting involves biology and has been used since the beginning of time to assist in procreation. It has been suggested by evolutionary biologists that those who flirted well were the most successful at finding mates and reproducing, and because of that, all humans attempted to adapt flirtatious behavior. We might not be limiting our flirtations to trying to find someone to procreate with, but we sure are using many of the innate techniques that have been in existence for centuries.

Getting it right is about tweaking the flirts to apply to a particular situation. Learning the art of the flirt when it comes to dating and relationships can make all the difference. It can help spice up a relationship you're already in, or help you connect with someone that you'd like to date. My goal is to provide you with a way to make connections that you didn't have before.

You'd be surprised at how many people believe that they cannot flirt. But the truth is—anyone can flirt! For some people, it's totally natural, and they've been flirtatious and charismatic their entire lives. For others it takes some practice, and I promise you, there is no shame in that. Anyone can become a good flirt—sometimes all it takes you getting out of your own way and learning a few tips and tricks.

When it comes to flirting amorously, there are really only five steps. Once you master them I guarantee that you will connect with people more easily both in the dating world and in every other facet of your life, too. You just need to learn when to turn it up and when to tone it down. Once you're aware of these steps and how to apply them in your daily life (because once you are a fearless flirt, flirting can take place anywhere and everywhere), you will see how easy it is to become comfortable with and good at flirting, and to connect with people.

To really be good at flirting—the main thing you have to watch out for, besides being in your own way, is *fear*. Fear is a primal drive, and it's one of the strongest emotions humans can experience. It can hold us back in almost all aspects of our lives, especially love. There is so much fear when it comes to flirting and dating! Fear of getting hurt, looking stupid, being rejected, falling in love, or making a bad impression...and those are just a few of our worries. In order to move forward you need to banish that fear, eliminating it completely, and the best way to do that is through knowledge. Knowledge and practice can eradicate the fear that's been holding you back from making meaningful connections. That's one of the things we are going to take care of in this book. The next eleven chapters will literally give you the map to help you find your inner flirt and unleash it on any object of your affection, without fear. You will learn where the best places are to get you flirt on, who you should recruit for your flirting offensive line, and what to do to when flirting situations get sticky. Watch out—there is a lot of info crammed into this little book!

All I ask is that you start with an open mind and remember to *have fun*. My goal in this book is to help everyone who reads this become a fearless flirt. I want you to have the tools and foundation to go out there and go after what you want, without fear. Sure, it isn't always going to be easy, and it might not always work exactly as you hoped, but if you approach the dating world with fearlessness and confidence, no one can stop you! The possibilities that can come your way as a result of being a fearless flirt are endless and really depend on what you are looking for. Do you want someone to date, fall in love with, or marry? Flirting can bring you all that and more. Just looking to have fun and make connections? Flirting will help you do that too. Flirting is really the gateway to any romantic experience you are looking to have, and will give you the tools to create the opportunity for those situations to occur, and cultivate those relationships.

1

Ready. Set. Go!

*"Before everything else, getting ready is
the secret of success."*
- Henry Ford

It would simply be wrong to start this book off with my surefire tips for becoming a super flirt. I mean, this is powerful stuff! You could practically take over the dating universe by implementing the nuggets in chapter 5. I need to make sure you are washed, waxed, and buffed first (and I mean that somewhat literally).

Quite frankly, there are some things that need to be addressed before you get out there and get your flirt on, things that can make or break you when you are looking to meet people to flirt with and date. Things that can either hold you back or propel you forward. These three things are *confidence, appearance and attitude.*

Without confidence in yourself you won't be able to approach people because you won't feel worthy of their attention.

Without looking your best, you may end up attracting people who are not at your level or who aren't your type.

Without the right attitude, you won't be able to keep an open mind and *have fun*!

Let's break these three pre-flirt focus areas down one by one, so you can make the most of your flirting experiences. And remember, dating and flirting are FUN. If you are not having fun, you're doing something wrong. Seek shelter and contact me immediately.

CONFIDENCE

"Accept who you are; and revel in it." - Mitch Albom,
Tuesdays with Morrie

Regardless of what anyone ever tells you, confidence is the single most important tool when it comes to flirting and dating. Confidence is what makes less-attractive people look like super-models! When you see a super-attractive woman walking down the street hand in hand with a markedly less attractive guy, do you just scratch your head? I guarantee you, 99% of the time that pairing exists because he has a massive amount of confidence in himself and what he has to offer in a relationship. I have a friend who will freely admit that she is not the most attractive woman alive. On a scale of 1 to 10, Pam is probably somewhere around a 6.5. She is overweight, needs a new wardrobe, and she almost always has to get her roots done. However, she has men fawning over her all the time. I kid you not—she can walk into a party and without fail will be asked out more than once. It is all because of her confidence. When Pam walks into that party she OWNS the room. Literally. She simply radiates confidence because regardless of any "flaws," she loves herself. Her self-regard is infectious and it's simply amazing to watch it in action.

Sadly, this mechanism works in reverse as well, and I have seen plenty of that. You may be gorgeous, but if you're insecure and lack confidence, it is going to severely hamper you in the dating world. I've known many people who truly have a ton to offer from the inside, and are attractive on the outside, but they cannot meet people because of a heartbreaking lack of confidence.

If you are not naturally confident, you need to change it up before you jump in the dating pool—and you can. You need to believe that you are flirt-worthy! When you look in the mirror you need to like what you see, and you need to like who you are. Those are the things that you need to own before you can begin to learn how to be flirty and fun. Some people already have all the confidence that's needed to get out there, and, as I said, other people need to work on it. That's totally cool! Confidence is something that you can work on, and you can even make it look like it comes naturally—even if you are continuing to put effort into it.

Flirting Tip #1

Confidence is key! Whether you have it, or need to get it—confidence is necessary when flirting.

Regardless of whether you just came out of a bad relationship, marriage, or a situation that brought you down, the first thing you need to do before you go back out on the market is to fall back in love with yourself. You can flirt with yourself! I'm going to show you that there are ways you can work on your confidence—without sitting on a therapist's couch for the next ten years.

Get Affirmed

One of my favorite things to do for myself is keep an affirmation handy. Whether you call it an affirmation or a mantra, it's a way of supporting and encouraging yourself, and it's something you should keep in your head to make you feel good and remind YOU of what you have to offer. It really can be anything, as long as it's positive and plausible. For example, I could tell myself daily that I look as good as a Victoria's Secret model, but I am not promoting being self-delusional here. But telling myself that I am smart and sexy? Now we're talking. I can believe that, and saying it and thinking it helps me to own it. No matter who you are, there is something that you like about yourself that you can remind yourself of whenever possible. Whether it has to do with your looks, your abilities, your huge heart or your immense brain, there is something you can focus on that you can own and believe. There are dozens, maybe even hundreds of qualities that people are looking for, and will look for in you! The positive self-beliefs that you hold can become a mantra for yourself to remind you of your value. So when you're getting ready to get your flirt on, create a mantra and run with it. Repeat that mantra to yourself every single day and remind yourself that *you are worthy of flirting!*

Sweat It Out

Another huge way to build your confidence is by raising your adrenaline and getting your sweat on. You don't have to be model-thin or have rock hard abs to flirt, but just getting your body moving and releasing those endorphins will make a huge difference in the way that you feel about yourself. There is something called a "cardio high" that I believe in, a thousand percent. When you do any cardio type of activity like running, walking, biking or dance, you literally feel high after the workout and for some time after. It pumps you up and it can make you feel invincible!

Working out on a regular basis can both change and extend your life. Consistency is key here. Start with a routine that you can maintain, and try to build up to working out at least three times a week, for at least 45 minutes. If the thought of sweating that much makes you queasy, take baby steps. Start with 30 minutes a couple of times a week—even if you are just walking. Anything you do to get started will be great, because once you see even the small effects of a little workout, you're going to be more motivated to add to it. Get to the gym, find a park to run around, go for a hike—just *move*. No matter where you are in the world or the resources you have available to you, there is always somewhere to get a workout going. Again, it is not about the resulting aesthetics here (although the repercussions of a workout can be a pretty sweet ass), but it's about getting your blood flowing, endorphins surging, and reminding yourself what you are capable of all on your own! You are guaranteed to feel better about yourself. I promise.

Eliminate Toxins

No, I am not telling you to do a juice fast or drink a ton of water. What I do want you to do is cleanse toxic *people* from your life. Think about this: it is a sad fact that misery loves company. There are people in this world who simply are not happy, and they resent people who are. Often, unless you take a step back and assess the situation, you may not realize that there may be people in your life who are destroying your confidence and bringing you down. NFL coach Vince Lombardi once said, "Confidence is contagious. So is a lack of confidence." Surrounding yourself by negative, unconfident people will not raise you up, but bring you down. Sometimes you let these people have power over you, the power to bring you down, because you feel as though they're "better" than you. *They're not*. People who put other people down are not better, in any way. Or you may be friends or spend time with these pathetic, negative people because you feel sorry for them—but I am here to tell you that right now, you need to take care of yourself first. This might be the hardest exercise in the book, but also the most rewarding. Take a moment to look around you and the people you surround yourself with. Ask yourself, "Are they lifting me up? Or bringing me down?" Your answer will dictate your action. Take the time to purposely surround yourself with people who are positive and encouraging. Life is too short to be less than happy!

GET FEARLESS

- Create your own specific affirmation—whisper sweet nothings…to yourself!

- Break a sweat—make a commitment to exercise at least three times per week.

- De-toxify—eliminate negative influencers and surround yourself with positivity!

APPEARANCE

"Beauty is only skin deep, but ugly goes clean to the bone." - Dorothy Parker

The world can be a judgmental place. For example, I'm sure you know that your looks will be evaluated the second you meet someone. It's a fact of life that there is a natural tendency for many to rate and judge others based on outward appearances—without knowing one iota about someone's personality. Humans are by nature visual creatures—and men are especially vulnerable to that instinct. It might seem shallow, but your first impression is pretty important! And of course, you only have one chance to make that first impression. I'm not saying that looks are everything, but it is important to work with what you have, and ignoring the way you present your physical self is just a mistake.

When someone starts coaching with me, the first thing we work on is appearance (as long as they give me a green light—otherwise it just seems mean to give someone my unsolicited opinion about how they look). Taking the time to make the most out of what you have is crucial before getting out there and look-ing to meet people. The truth of the matter is this: when you know you look good, you will feel good—and that confidence we talked about earlier will come naturally.

You can look hotter no matter what your starting point is. And it's not hard to do.

1. **Clean it up.** This seems a little basic, no? But you would be surprised how many people think it's okay to go out right after the gym, without showering. Staying clean and fresh isn't that hard, and it is completely economical. A bar of soap (and some water) is all you need. Guys, this includes your hands and nails. We love a manly man who gets his hands dirty, but we like him even better when he is all cleaned up.

2. **Smell nice, but not too nice.** This is technically "appear-ance," but your scent can help make you less or more attractive. There are thousands of perfumes and colognes on the market that are supposed to make you appeal to

the opposite sex, but please be aware that they don't work on overload. Find a scent you like and use it sparingly.

3. **Wear makeup.** Makeup can go a long way towards turning a semi-attractive woman into a total hottie. Even for the lowest maintenance women, a little concealer, lip gloss, and mascara can work magic. Many women truly have no idea how to apply makeup. Do yourself a favor if you're one of them—go get help. Find a Sephora or a high-end salon in your area and ask for a makeup application and lesson—most salons and spas offer this service. Trained professionals will know how to apply the makeup in the right colors to bring out your "natural beauty," and they'll also know how to explain it you, so that you'll be able to apply the same kind of makeup yourself. It's worth the investment of time and money. (For ladies only. Sorry, guys, no lip gloss for you.)

4. **Do your hair.** When you're going out, whether you are male or female it doesn't matter—please, put a little more effort in. It doesn't take that much to run a brush through your hair or use whatever tool can help show off your hair in the best possible condition. Find a style that looks nice on you and run with it. If you haven't changed your hair in the last decade or if you're unsure if your 'do is still working for you, I again plead with you to seek professional help. Ask for a recommendation and see a stylist to help you find your best look. Yelp.com is an amazing resource for finding salons and stylists in your area that

have already been vetted (as well as all sorts of other services). Here's my mantra for you: You are worth it!

5. **Ditch the sweatpants.** Do not go out in sweatpants if you are looking to meet someone new! This also goes for clothing with holes (unless they are intentional) or stains. Your clothing can make or break your chances at making a great first impression! I want you to be comfortable, but I also want you to look good! Here are some key tips that you should keep in mind regarding flirty fashions:

Ladies:

- Show some skin, but not too much. If you wear a short skirt, keep the top modest. If you wear a sexy shirt, make sure that the bottom compliments by not being too revealing. I love a sexy halter or low-cut top with jeans and heels, but it is really about what works on YOU.

- Make sure it fits! Do not live or die by the tag. Designers cut their clothes differently from each other, so a size 10 isn't always a size 10, for example. A good fit goes a long way.

- Start from the bottom up. A sexy bra and panty combo will provide the right foundation for a fun and flirty frame of mind.

- Do you have a great LBD? A little black dress is a staple, and can be a go-to pick for almost any occasion.

Guys:

- Cleanliness is next to Godliness. Go beyond the sniff test and *make sure* everything you wear is actually clean.

- Keep it simple. There is nothing more attractive than a pair of jeans or khakis and a button-down. Simple is sexy.

- Check the kicks. Sometimes your shoes can be a little worse for the wear, and they'll very likely be noticed. Buff them if you can; if not, invest in a new pair.

- Go blue! (And I don't necessarily mean Michigan.) Still not sure what to wear? Pick something blue. Studies have shown that blue is the most attractive to women.

As always, you should never be afraid to ask for help with getting any of this done. Most department stores are filled with associates who would be more than happy to offer their expert opinions and give you a hand. If you want to take it a step further, there are stylists nationwide who offer complete makeovers. I am talking TV-worthy-raid-your-closet-and-take-you-shopping experiences. If your finances allow it, I guarantee that this kind of makeover is an experience that will pay off tenfold, with lots of dividends, especially in the confidence that looking your best will give you.

Flirting Tip #2

Look good and smell nice (or vice versa!). When in doubt phone a friend, or a professional, to get help!

This advice might have seemed utterly shallow, and I agree completely—it does appeal to the superficial! However, there is no shame in putting a bit of effort into making you *the best* you. What is inside is what truly matters, but if we can get you looking as good on the outside as you are amazing on the inside, you will be unstoppable!

GET FEARLESS

- Remember appearances count, but confidence is key—raise your confidence by feeling like you look your best.
- Keep it clean and simple.
- Know when to call in backup—professional makeup artists and stylists abound and can make sure you are putting your best foot forward.

ATTITUDE

"Attitude is a little thing that makes a big difference."
-Winston Churchill

We have been indoctrinated in the belief that there is power in positive thinking, that life is about putting mind over matter, and that you can literally change your future by changing your attitude. Well—I am here to confirm that it is all true, even when it comes to flirting.

Positivity is intoxicating. There are people in my life that I love to surround myself with simply because they are always happy and looking on the bright side. It is inspiring and always works to lift my spirits when I am not feeling so optimistic myself. On the flip side, negativity can be a black hole in your dating life. That negativity can have just as powerful of an impact. There are so many instances where your own attitude could be getting in your way of making connections with people. Take this true story about one of my clients, Reese:

> *Reese was a smart, attractive, divorced 42-year-old woman looking to find someone to spend her life with—or at least date! Her divorce had taken a lot out of her and she spent almost two years afterwards in counseling, working on rebuilding her confidence. She became tired of being alone and decided to "get back out there," so she hit the bar scene and put up a profile on Match.com. In spite of her proactive measures, Reese was still not making connections and was becoming increasingly frustrated.*
>
> *What Reese didn't realize was that the problem was herself! Reese was convinced that online dating didn't work. Reese was convinced that you could never meet anyone decent in a bar. Reese also believed deep down that all men were going to disappoint her, just like her ex-husband did. Even though it looked like she was making all the right moves, her attitude was terrible! That attitude prevented the real Reese from shining through, whether she met people online or off.*
>
> *After several coaching sessions, Reese was finally able to recognize her poor attitude and make a conscious effort to turn it around. At first it felt fake to her, but she put a smile*

on and banished any negative thoughts. Eventually she started to believe in the possibility of something good happening, because of the reaction she got from men as a result of her new outlook. Reese is now happily dating a man she met at a networking event, who later told her he was initially attracted to her warm and inviting personality!

Seriously, people, attitude is everything! Take a look at yourself. Are you happy? If not, why not? That is the first question you need to answer. If there is something you can change, than change it. If not, you have to change the way you look at it.

Positivity when flirting and dating is absolutely essential. No one wants to date Debbie Downer! I am not telling you it has to be puppies and rainbows 24/7, but it better be pure sunshine at least through your initial flirtations! People are naturally attracted to those with a good attitude. Not the happiest camper in the bunch? Don't worry—there are ways for you to get that right attitude and show it off!

Flirting Tip #3

The right attitude will carry you for miles. Change your attitude and change your future.

And getting the right attitude is half the battle, especially if you have things in your life that are bringing you down. Divorce, breakups, toxic friends, and bad bosses are some of the things that can kill your positivity and put you in a negative space. But take note of these three steps that can help bring you back to your happy place.

1. **Think happy thoughts**—Literally. Push negativity out of your head. Focus on the positive parts of your day, and the brightness of your future.

2. **Eliminate negative people**—We talked about this in the section on confidence, but it is worth repeating. Negativity is contagious. Have a friend with a bad attitude about dating, or about men (or women) in general? Leave Mr. or Ms. Negatory behind when you go out networking, to a mixer or even just to the local bar. When you are going out, bring a fun and flirty POSITIVE friend who can help keep you in the right frame of mind—because positivity is contagious too. If I've said it once, I've said it a thousand times: flirting and dating are fun!

3. **Fake it until you make it**—Take a lesson from Reese: she wasn't fully on board, but she put a smile on her face, focused on the positive, and eventually her "fake" became *real*.

Once you have the right attitude, it is all about showing it off! You probably have no idea how completely attractive positivity can be. Here are three steps for showing the rest of the world that you have the right attitude.

1. **Smile and laugh**—Those pearly whites do wonders. *Really*. Smiling shows that you are happy—it sends a signal to other people's brains that you are positive and approachable. Laughing is even better. Genuine laughter is an amazing way to show people that you are fun!

2. **Talk about positive things**—Leave negativity out of conversations and online profiles. Don't complain about your exes, your job or your life in general until you get to know each other a little better. Focus on the good things that you have to offer.

3. **Keep your eyes, ears and heart open**—With the right attitude you will be open to opportunities that may not be what you had originally wanted, but might be what you actually need. Say *yes* more than *no*, keep an open mind and heart, and you may be surprised and delighted at what comes your way.

A good attitude can make or break your love life. Expending a little effort focused on opening your mind to what the world has to offer will make flirting and connecting a breeze. Stay positive, and show it!

GET FEARLESS

- Remember that a positive attitude can change your present and your future.

- Don't be afraid to work on changing your perspective, or at least faking it until you make it.

- Once you have it, don't be afraid to flaunt it!

2

Where to Get Your Flirt On

*"Opportunity dances with those already
on the dance floor."*
- H. Jackson Brown, Jr

*"***W***hy doesn't she like me? What should I wear on my date? How can I ask her out? Why are all the good guys taken, or gay? How much chest hair is too much?* Of all those questions (most of which you'll find answers to throughout the book), my least favorite question is, *"Where do I go to meet people?"*

Why is this my least favorite question? Because if you are in the right frame of mind, and have the tools I give you in this book, you can meet people EVERYWHERE! I literally mean *everywhere*. I don't care whether you're at the dry cleaner, the grocery store, in a subway, a bar, at an airport, a park, or the dog groomer—you can get your flirt on there. As long as there are people, there is opportunity. It is all about keeping your eyes open and embracing opportunities.

Of course, there are places and situations that are more conducive to flirting than others, and spots that are better than others for meeting singles. Flirting at a funeral might not be entirely appropriate (although I have seen it done), and there are circumstances where people will be more receptive to your flirtations. For that reason, I am going to rephrase the "Where do I go to meet people?" question, so it's:

"What are the BEST places to meet people?"

Options exist everywhere you look, but they are not all created equal. A bar is always going to be better than the subway, because of the frame of mind people are in while they're there. On the subway people are on the move, they are going to work, to an appointment, home at the end of a long day—they are headed toward a specific destination, and that may be occupying their mind. But at a bar, people are looking to relax and to meet other people. Sure you can flirt on the subway, but you will have to overcome much less resistance at a bar. If you're in the right frame of mind, and you're flirting with others in the right frame of mind, you can hit a home run. (You will see that "frame of mind" is a recurring theme in this book, for very good reasons.)

Is the neighborhood bar losing its luster? Some flirters also need to be reminded that variety can be the spice of life! Maybe your go-to places aren't working for you. You might be comfortable there, but your possibilities are far from endless. Everyone needs to learn to switch it up sometimes to keep your energy up and prospects wide. We're all creatures of habit, but if you've been going to the same places for the past ten years and have yet to meet anyone flirt-worthy, you might want to consider changing the scenery. Take Michael....

Michael came to consult with me when he was 45 years old, after coming out of a 10-year marriage. He regularly worked long hours as an emergency room physician in a major city hospital, and rarely felt comfortable flirting with anyone he met through work (gunshot wounds really don't set the mood). Feeling lonely, Michael used his limited free time to try and get back in the dating game. However, Michael was a creature of habit.

Every single Saturday night he wasn't working, Michael always went to the same bar/restaurant. Sure, it was a nice place, but it was a local crowd, and the patrons were mostly couples. He sat in the same seat. He talked to the same people. He ended up spending more time talking to the same old bartenders than meeting new people. Michael did meet one *woman there who he went out with for a little while, but it fizzled pretty quickly after they realized they had nothing in common other than they both liked their martinis dirty (who doesn't love gin, vermouth, olives, and a splash of olive juice?). But Michael kept on trucking, never switching it up, and continued to keep his barstool warm every Saturday. He continued to drink his dirty martinis alone (with the company of the bartender), but failed to meet anyone new who was interesting enough to date. A simple move to the bar down the street could have made all the difference, but he was in a committed relationship—with the Ravenwood. *Shockingly* he was still single when he signed up for one of my dating boot camps where he learned what he was doing wrong, and his options for fixing it.*

Do you have a little Michael in you? Are you a creature of habit? Do you go to the same place over and over, and then you're surprised that new people don't magically appear? It's all too easy to end up in that situation; familiarity can be tempting because it's comforting. So sometimes you just need to be reminded of your options. Read on for a list that is going to help you to find new places, where you can meet new people—people who have (drum roll, please)—the right frame of mind!

Flirting Tip #4

Look outside the box when thinking about places to meet people. You can flirt anywhere!

When you want to pick the BEST places to flirt, you can now check out the following top ten non-dating focused options, and another five purely dating-related choices. I would actually prefer for you to focus on the non-dating suggestions. These locations and their related opportunities take the pressure off because everyone is not going to have a one-track mind focused on meeting the love of their life (or the love of their night), and instead, the focus is on the fun. However, I am all about hedging your bets, so I suggest you pick a few from each list and get out there!

NOT SO MUCH DATING

Here's a list of 10 places you might not have thought about. They aren't the "typical" locations that would come to mind when you think about picking someone up, but can be just as (or even more) fruitful. I think they are even better *because* they are atypical. One, because with most of them you will have fun regardless of whether or not you find someone to flirt with, and two, there is zero "I'm single—talk to me? Please?" pressure. Sure, some of them will have both singles and attached people in attendance, but they are all good places to practice your flirt skills. Just keep an open mind, and remember to have fun.

1. Meetup.com

Meetup.com is the single greatest resource available today for meeting people (hence the name). There are literally thousands of groups in every part of the world. This is somewhat of a hybrid suggestion: singles groups abound on the site, but I want you to think outside the box. Check out the groups on Meetup.com that cater to things you are already interested in, even if the groups aren't specifically enlisting singles-only. You can join a group that hikes, surfs, takes photos, eats, speaks French, dresses up in Star Trek costumes (yes, that's what some people like to do!) or any other group activity, *and* possibly find a date. In any group you choose, through your common interest you'll have an immediate connection with these formerly complete strangers, which makes flirting that much easier! Sure, some of them may not be single, but many will be. Also, never underestimate the power of making new friends—your group members may be the ones to lead you to Mr. or Ms. Right. It becomes a win-win all around!

2. LivingSocial/Groupon

No, I'm not telling you to buy $45 worth of waxing for $20 (unless you need it), but you should be signed up for at least LivingSocial and Groupon in your area and surrounding cities. These coupon sites are chock-full of fun experiences! Livingsocial.com actually has a whole tab dedicated to "Adventures." Right now in the New York City area there are options to go whitewater rafting, wine tasting, kayaking, river tubing, or hitting up an '80s party. All in a group where you can meet people, and at a discount! Grab a fun friend (preferably your wingman or wingwoman—see chapter 3) and sign up, or go solo! Again, the focus is on the fun!

3. Business Networking

Who says you can't mix business with pleasure? Maybe it's not a good idea to flirt incessantly with your officemate (unless your company allows it, they are a willing participant, and your work won't be affected. Heck, that's a whole other book...), but what about all those events your boss makes you attend? Those are prime avenues for getting your flirt on! Where else will you find like-minded, employed, and ambitious people in one room? Similar to other non-singles scenes, not everyone will be available, but with 96 million single people in the United States alone, there will definitely be some who are unattached. Make an attempt to meet everyone you can! Focus on business, but don't be afraid to also make a personal connection, if you see that it's appropriate.

4. Seminars/Conferences

If your seminars or conferences are business-related, what you just read about business networking applies. However, not all seminars and conferences are related to work, so this deserves separate mention. At these meetings you'll encounter a group of like-minded individuals focused on a topic (whether it be business, cultural, creative, or social) that will provide you with a safe place to start conversations and make connections. I had a client who met her husband at a weekend creative writing workshop—they built a strong foundation for their relationship based on their mutual passion for becoming published authors. They now have a built-in editor in their partner, and a happy marriage that goes far beyond their manuscripts.

5. Airports

I have met more people in airports than almost anywhere else. I'd like to think it's my warm and inviting personality that was responsible for making the connections, but I think it's more because I had a captive audience. Literally. The people I meet in airports have nowhere to run, unless they want the TSA to tackle them, so they might as well talk to me. Whether they're initially interested or not, we always end up having great conversations, and we often become friends beyond the terminals. Airports are filled with thousands of people forced to waste time, so go mingle! Whether it is due to layovers, flight delays, cancellations, or unexpectedly short lines at security (wait, that never happens), there are often thousands mulling about to talk to. The airport bars are clearly the easiest location, but don't overlook the waiting areas that also house people desperate to pass the time with conversation.

6. Hotel Bars

Next to airports, hotel bars are one of the easiest places to start conversations. Frankly, bars in general seem to do the trick here, but when a solo traveler heads down to the bar in his or her hotel, the element of familiarity is removed and it almost forces people to move outside of their comfort zone and start conversations. Solo travelers can get lonely and can be a very engaging audience under the right circumstances. So next time you are traveling, head down to the bar for a beer or martini—you never know who you will meet!

7. Gyms

I typically don't recommend gyms as places to flirt, because frankly, I become a sweaty mess when I work out and I am never feeling super flirty at the gym. However, it's not about me, it's about *you*, and you may feel completely different about this. Also, whether or not *you* feel flirty at the gym, plenty of other people *definitely* do! For that reason, the gym is a *must* location to check out when looking to check people out. Gyms are literally filled with single people trying to get in shape (or the lucky ones are trying to *stay* in shape) to look their best. So if you don't look and feel gross (like me) when you work out, sign up for a gym and get yourself there during peak after-work hours. It's amazing the conversations you can start on adjacent ellipticals.

8. Dog Parks

The prerequisite for this as a good meeting place is: you have to have a dog. Showing up at a dog park *sans* dog and ogling dog owners is just weird. Don't have a dog? Borrow one and head on over. Most of the time the owners are alone with their dogs, which makes starting a conversation even easier. You already know that you have a mutual interest, which as you have seen elsewhere, always leads to a greater chance of success! Plus, my grandmother always said that people who love pets are good people to know. (I miss my grandma—she was a tough cookie, but she sure had some great words of wisdom.)

9. Church/Temple/Mosque

Obviously meeting at a house of worship will not appeal to everyone, but I would be remiss if I didn't put it on the list. For the religious crowd, there is probably no greater place to meet people than the church/temple/mosque that you belong to. If yours is anything like the church I grew up in, it is filled with sometimes overbearing nonprofessional marriage brokers looking to match up singles in the congregation. Either way, you get your faith in, and might even get your flirt on. Just not during the service, please; I don't want to get yelled at by your pastor.

10. Starbucks (or any similar coffee shop)

Last but not least on my top ten list is your favorite coffee shop. I love Starbucks, personally. It has a great, almost sexy vibe to it with music, plush furniture pushed too close together, and my favorite thing in the world, caffeine. The only problem with Starbucks is that people tend to get in their zone once they sit down. Don't fret, though! A strategic spot on line will give you all the opportunity you need to find a coffee addict just like you. It can often lead to an instant date when the two of you pick up your *venti soy mocha latte no-whip extra shot* and sit down to chat.

Now you can see that you don't have to go to a singles event to meet people! There are singles everywhere, and the shortcut to finding people you want to flirt with is finding that common denominator. Having something in common off the bat makes approaching, connecting and conversing that much easier.

GET FEARLESS

- Be open to flirting opportunities everywhere you go.

- Find a place that works for you, and has your interests as a focal point.

- Get out of the house as often as possible. Try new things. Spend a month saying "Yes" to every opportunity that your friends invite you to.

SINGLES-FOCUSED

Sometimes you just want to go straight for the bulls-eye. You don't want to waste time weeding through the married, attached or otherwise engaged—you want 'em primed and ready! Below are my top five suggestions for places to get your flirt on with other singles.

1. Online

Online dating is the single largest meeting place in the world for singles. There are millions looking for love online. At its inception fifteen years ago, online dating was considered taboo by most, and was often seen as something that only desperate people would use. However, during the last decade, things have changed drastically in terms of the public's perception. Almost everyone that you know now knows someone who met and married their spouse through an online dating website. Forty million Americans say that they have tried at least one online dating site! If you are single and you're interested in meeting people, you need to be online. Period.

I'm not saying that online dating is not often frustrating, because it can be. Frankly, there are a lot of things that online dating has failed to address to meet the needs of its users. I started FlipMe.com because of frustrated online daters who were sick of having no chemistry with their dates, either because of inaccurate profiles or flat-out false personas. A short digression here for those who aren't familiar with FlipMe—these are flirt cards (real tangible cards) that allow women to make the first move without giving out their personal information. Users get a deck of cards, each with a flirty phrase on the front and a unique code on the back that connects the member and the recipient of the card through the website. The goal was to focus on attraction and the chemistry you have when you first see or meet someone. It's designed as a fun way to break the ice. Okay, commercial over.

Just because I created FlipMe doesn't mean I don't believe in online dating in general—I do. I am hopeful, though, that the powers that be are working to make it a better experience for users. Like I said, there is no other larger resource for singles out there that matches the accessibility, number of singles publicly "labeled" as being available, and options that online dating has to offer, and because of that, it cannot be ignored.

Something else that can't be ignored? Tips and tricks for dating online. Before I send you into a sea of thousands of singles, there are some hints, tips and rules that you should check out before you click "Join."

Tips for Flirting Online

Once you pick your poison, er, your favorite site(s), there are a few things we need to discuss before you publish that profile. Here are my top ten tips for flirting online.

1. **Put up a photo**—Profiles with photos get twice as many responses. People are visual, and the first thing most users consider are your pictures. Do me a favor, and *please* make it a recent picture. Inaccurate or deceptive photos are one of the top reasons why users of online dating sites get frustrated. Don't take good pictures? Hire a professional—there are thousands of photographers that now offer "online dating photo packages." It isn't cheating—it is just showing you in your best light.

2. **Keep your photos "safe"**—Do not post half-naked photos of yourself and don't market yourself in provocative poses. This will set a tone that you might not be aiming for. Yes, we all like to look and feel sexy, but online there is no "context." We might not realize that you are both sexy AND smart/deep/spiritual from a

picture, and will likely put you immediately into the casual sex/slutty category. Play it safe.

3. **Stay positive**—Do not talk about anything negative in your profile. Focus on the positive! Talk about the fun things you like to do, the places you've been, and what you have to offer.

4. **Keep it short**—Brevity is key when it comes to online dating profiles. Do not ramble on for ten paragraphs. This is especially important if you're a woman looking for a man—most men will look at your pictures and then skim the written portion. If you go on for days about your cats or how much you love ice cream, you are going to get passed over.

5. **Flirt as if you were face to face**—Your online communications should have the same tone as your offline chats. Be fun and flirty, pay compliments, and use humor (if you are funny).

6. **Do not mention marriage**—The words "marriage" or "soul mate" should never be included in an online dating profile. Nothing scares people more than: "I can't wait to get married" or "Looking for my soul mate." Sure, you can think it, but just don't write it.

7. **Do not use all caps to talk, and check your spelling**—This may seem like nitpicking, but an online first impression is 10 times harsher than in person. You can be clicked over in a heartbeat, and you would be surprised

how attractive a good speller can be. All caps? Never
pretty. No one wants to be yelled at.

8. **Make a date ASAP**—Meet in person as quickly as you
feel comfortable. Do not spend months falling in love
with a profile—you need to meet in person to make sure
you have enough chemistry to move forward. The biggest
complaint I hear about online dating is inaccurate
profiles. Men often lie about their height, women about
their age, and both put up pictures that look nothing like
them. I once met a guy who said he was 6'3", but he
barely reached my chin. I am 5'8". Get all of those issues
out of the way off the bat so you can see if there is a real
connection.

9. **Keep an open mind**—Try not to expand your "must
have" list just because the site gives you more dropdown
boxes to choose from. Remember that chemistry accounts
for a lot, and while he or she may not be "perfect," they
could make one hell of a date. Take a chance once or
twice and meet someone you wouldn't typically date—
you might be surprised. One cup of coffee won't kill you,
and as a matter of fact, you might even stay for dessert.

10. **Don't get attached too quickly**—Online dating is a
kind of window-shopping, where everyone is browsing.
Make sure you know that no one is committed until both
parties say so, and understand that you may see your
new crush online continuing to search. It doesn't mean
they don't want to still see if there is a connection with

you. It's probably because they haven't met you yet, and don't realize how fabulous you are.

Finding the Right Fit

Before you go and sign up at 17 different dating websites, I do have to warn you that there are thousands of sites out there, and each has its own pros and cons. There are more than 1,500 sites in the United States alone. So I'm going to give you a short list of the ones that I'm familiar with and comfortable recommending.

New dating sites pop up all the time, and there is a site for almost every niche imaginable, so if there is one you see that looks like it's for you—check it out! Many of the sites are free, so you can sign up, search around, and get the feel before you even put up a profile. Do some research online and check out reviews. The beauty of the internet is that there are millions of people giving their opinions on anything and everything, including dating sites. Google the name of the site and "reviews" and you are guaranteed hours of reading material. You can also ask friends what sites they have used, if you feel comfortable. Finding a site that feels right will drastically improve your dating experience, so test out a few. Most paid sites have a free trial or at least a limited free membership, so you can check out the users and then sign up once you see if the site could work for you. My recommendations in some particular order are as follows:

> **Match.com**—Match.com is the online dating giant. They have more users than almost any other site, which means you have more options for possible dates. It also means you have to dig through a ton of people to find ones that pique your interest. It's a paid site, but worth the money

if you are truly interested in meeting someone. The age range is pretty broad, covering those just newly of dating age through the nursing home years. A bonus with Match.com is a recently launched series of offline events called the Stir. These events are designed to bring members together "in real life" to meet and mingle at venues nationwide. If I were going to sign up for one site only, it would probably be Match.com, and I would definitely take advantage of attending those member-only events.

OkCupid—OkCupid is on the rise, and is definitely one of the more "fun" online dating sites around. The site is FREE and it's very easy to use. Its algorithm (the way the site matches you) includes your answers to some very probing questions, some very funny questions, and some very off-the-wall questions. You could spend the rest of your life answering OkCupid's questions, but the beauty of it is that you don't have to (although you should answer at least a few to get the matching system fired up). The site tends to trend younger, so I wouldn't recommend OkCupid if you are over 50.

eHarmony—eHarmony focuses on serious long-term relationships. It was started by a Christian psychologist focused on marriage, and initially, eHarmony only allowed heterosexual couples, but thereafter spun off a corresponding site for same-sex couples (Compatible Partners). I often recommend this site for my mature clients not looking to "just date." Its questionnaire to sign up (which I believe is currently 250+ questions) can be a doozy, and you cannot just search for people—they have to be sent to you based on mutual compatibility. Nevertheless it provides a great forum to meet like-minded people who are looking for something more intense.

Plenty of Fish—PlentyofFish.com is another free site, which is great, and it has tons of members. Its members also encompass a wide range of ages so it is a great option for anyone looking to add a free site to their dating-base repertoire. It can be somewhat difficult to navigate, especially with the multitude of members, but if you have the time to spend navigating, it can be 100% worth it.

Howaboutwe—I like Howaboutwe.com because the site doesn't match you, it makes you get off the computer and meet each other. Instead of filling out massive profiles, you suggest a date, and if someone likes your suggestion, you move offline and get together. It's a fun way to meet people quickly who like to do the same things you do. Just reading all of the dates that people suggest on the site is entertaining. There is everything from "Let's go to a wine tasting," to "Wanna go see a movie?" to "Let's play doctor." You might need to weed through a bunch before you find something that appeals to you. If you are planning on suggesting a date, make it specific. Suggest going to eat a certain dish at a restaurant in your area, or catching a free concert coming up. Make it specific enough to stand out, but avoid "Let's skip the date and

just make out on my couch…at my parent's house…
where I still live."

There are literally thousands of other sites out there that I am
sure can do the trick. Many of the niche sites (JDate.com, Our-
Time.com, etc.) are good options for those looking to zoom in on
a certain sector of the dating public. Just as a side note, even on
the niche sites, there will be members that are outside of the "target." I personally know many non-Jewish singles who are members of JDate, and I know many younger singles (under 40) who
are signed up on OurTime—so even these "specific" sites will take
some weeding through search results. I suggest signing up for at
least one paid site and one free site. I also suggest having no more
than 3 memberships at a time. You simply will not have the time
to give each membership the right amount of attention to get the
most out of the site. In a perfect world you will spend 30-60 minutes per day searching and emailing members on each site. Spending that amount of time on 5 sites could become a full-time job.
Try a site even for a month, even just to practice flirting and communicating on unsuspecting online guinea pigs, er, *people*.

Flirting Tip #5

*Keep your online presence completely positive. You
have precious seconds to make an impression.*

2. Speed Dating

Let's talk about speed dating events. Speed dating has been around for quite some time, and was allegedly invented by a Los Angeles rabbi based on a Jewish tradition of getting groups of singles together. It got a bad rap for a while, and wasn't exactly seen as something the "cool kids" were doing. However, in recent years speed dating has been making a comeback. This type of dating has also spawned a platonic version through business networking. One of my most efficient networking events as a businesswoman was a speed networking event—you were FORCED to meet everyone. It was great and it got you out of the typical cliques that form even at work-related events. I personally think the success of speed dating may be due to the fact that some have become frustrated with online dating and are looking for a different way to connect in person—but quickly and efficiently.

Nevertheless, speed dating is a fantastic way to meet singles. The best part about speed dating is that you don't have to put any effort into the approach, other than looking your best! In fact, there is no approach, whatsoever, there's no possibility of (immediate) rejection, and you don't even have to buy anyone a drink. All you have to do is sit in front of your speedy date and make conversation for as little as 60 seconds. There are tons of speed-dating opportunities across the country and a quick Google search can locate many options in and around your metro area.

If you are going to give it a shot, you should go to at least two speed dating events before deciding if it's for you. Many of the events are age-specific, but I have also seen some that are focused on interests. The best part about a speed dating event is that you can fine-tune your flirting pretty quickly when you are talking to that many people in one night!

3. Singles Events

Singles events take place in almost every area of the country, and you could really spend a lifetime going to them. Simply do a search for "singles events" and your metro area, and you're guaranteed to come up with thousands of hits leading you to a variety of events that are held by corporations, organizations, or individuals. As mentioned in the prior section, Meetup.com is also a great resource to find singles events near you.

Singles events are great ways to meet people because, one, everyone is single, and, two, they are normally centered around some sort of interest or hobby. Whether or not you want to make events that are completely focused on singles a large part of what makes up your dating pie is up to you.

4. Singles Cruises

Singles cruises used to be abundant, but the number of these kinds of parties have decreased significantly. However, there are still cruise lines that cater to singles and sites that put together groups of singles to go on cruises as a group, such as singlescruise. com. This is a great option for someone who is looking to mix vacation with a little love-searching. It doesn't mean you are going to end up in a long-term committed relationship (is there ever a guarantee?), but I will say that flirting on a boat in the Caribbean with a piña colada in hand doesn't seem like a bad way to practice your flirt skills.

I typically suggest a singles cruise to someone who is both in need of a vacation, and is looking to get back in the game after a breakup or divorce. It's almost like a jumpstart in terms of meeting people, but you can have a lot of fun at the same time. Regardless of what comes from it, you always have that amazing vacation!

5. Matchmaker

This one is slightly cheating (but in a good way). Matchmakers are not exactly a location to meet singles, but they do have offices, so I consider that contributing validity! Matchmakers are one of the single most amazing, underutilized resources related to dating. They literally take all the vetting work off the table and put you in front of people who you are most likely to connect with. It is a fantastic service for people who are simply too busy to go through these fourteen options. It is also a great resource for those who have tried other ways of meeting people, but have been unsuccessful.

The beauty of a matchmaker is that the matchmaker knows you! They know what you like and they screen everyone before you go out with them. That way you will know exactly what you are getting into, which is especially helpful for those who don't have the time to date a ton of people to find *the one*. Not interested in paying a matchmaker to set you up? You don't have to just write them off—you can sign up to be in their database. Most matchmakers offer a free membership to their site/database. If

Flirting Tip #6

Explore all options to meet people—online and off. Put up a profile and attend at least one event per week.

they have a client that you would be perfect for, you could get set up for free. It really can be a win-win.

As you can see, there are an enormous number of places and ways to meet people. In addition to these 15 suggestions, there is an infinite world of other opportunities for connecting with and meeting singles. The important thing is to get out there. You need to be going to at least one off-line event per week, and also using online dating as the fantastic tool that it is. This isn't just to force you to go out and meet people, but to force you to really fine-tune your skills at flirting and connecting with people. The more you do it, the better you will become at flirting. The better flirt you are, the better connections you will make. So make a list of the options that you feel most comfortable with and get on it! Get out there and go get 'em, tiger!

GET FEARLESS

- Get online—pick a site that fits your personality and put up that profile, already!

- Check out events in your area that appeal to your interests, and where you can find like-minded potential dates.

- Sign up for a matchmaker, or at least sign up to be in their database—who knows where it will lead?

3
Your Right-Hand Wingman (or Wingwoman)

"You can be my wingman any time."
- Iceman

Your friends can hold the keys to your flirting success, making it easier than you could ever imagine. Well, the *right* friends can, at least. A wingman or wingwoman can make all the difference in your flirting game, and give you the confidence to take chances and put yourself out there more than ever. A little more shy than most? Not sure how to approach people? Know how to approach but just don't want to do it? Wingman to the rescue! Your wingman can make introductions, offer you support and encouragement, and if necessary, keep you in check. They are an essential accessory for the shy, and an added bonus for the extroverted.

The concept of a wingman is not new; it has just become more popular recently. The term originated from the days of the early flying fighter planes. In aerial combat, the job of your wingman was to keep you safe and cover you in a dogfight, kind of like in dating, right? (Thankfully, dating is a bit safer and somewhat less stressful.) People have been using their friends to help them flirt and date for decades. From youth through adulthood, our friends have been a part of our flirtations. Remember grammar school? Friends were key players when it came time for passing scribbled notes that said, "Do you like me? Yes or No" to the guy across the room … or when your buddy would tell a girl that you thought she was cute. Having a wingman (or wingwoman) is a time-honored tradition. Frankly, I still witness men who approach women with the "My friend thinks you are cute" line. Some things never change…and while I don't recommend it, sometimes the grammar school charm still works.

Beyond keeping you on track and in check (more on this later), what's the bonus of flirting with friends? Guaranteed fun.

It is so much more fun to go out and meet people when you have a friend who is in the same frame of mind along for the ride. When you're having fun with your wingman, people will be naturally attracted to you. Simply put: people are attracted to fun. The more fun that you look like you're having, the more people will want to join in the fun with you. Try, though, to limit your group to two or three of you. It can be fairly intimidating for anyone to approach a group of more than three fun people.

There are two rules when flirting with a wingman at your side: 1) Choose your wingman wisely, and 2) always have a plan. If you cover both of those bases, you are set.

CHOOSING YOUR WINGED FRIEND

You may have many friends that you love dearly, but not all of them will make good wingmen. Choosing the right friends to hang out with when you're looking to get your flirt on is critical. There are certain qualities that a good wingman needs to have to make them effective for you, and remember, this is all about you here! You are the one looking to get flirty and meet people, and selecting the right person to go out with you can make that happen. Don't worry, you can make it up to them by being their wingman the next time. Teamwork is the name of the game!

You also need to remember that one of the ways you will be judged is based on your friends. Make sure the people you are hanging out with reflect the image you want to portray. They need to represent the personality traits that you want to show to your potential flirtations. (More about who to specifically *leave home* later…)

Let's talk about the top five qualities that you need to look for when picking your wingman or wingwoman:

1. **Trustworthy and committed**—Make sure you can trust her to stay with you, and stay on track. Can you trust her not to disappear? Can you trust her to back off when necessary? That girl you're constantly afraid is going to ditch you and go home with the first guy she meets is *not* a good wingwoman.

2. **Single**—I am not saying that you cannot use your attached friends as wingmen, but singles are much more effective for many reasons. One of the most important and practical reasons is that your attached friends may not have the patience to let you work your magic. The last thing you want is pointed, probing looks from your wingman indicating that you should wrap it up so he can continue complaining to you about his wife… or so he can get home to her early. If your wingman is single he is in a similar frame of mind to you, and knows what he needs to do to help you to shine.

3. **Fun**—As mentioned above, fun is hot! It is so attractive to see happy people having fun. Pick a friend who is fun and goes with the flow. Have a funny friend? Even better. Laughter is contagious and can draw people in to talk to you like flies to honey. (Remember what Grandma said— you will always catch more flies with honey.) Who *doesn't* like to laugh?

4. **Selfless**—Your wingwoman needs to be completely focused on you—at least for the night! She needs to recognize that her role is to help you. You get first choice, and she needs to play a supporting role. Her job is to keep an eye out for you, keep an eye on you, and keep herself in check. Impaired or wasted wingwomen tend not to be effective. That doesn't mean she can't have fun and meet people too—she just needs to put you first (for only a few hours).

5. **Aware**—Make sure your wingman knows you well enough to know your type and read your cues. That way they know who to be on the lookout for, when to back off, or when to come in and save you!

If you can find someone with these qualities to be your wingman you will be flying high, and have all the backup you need to have a fun flirty night. Please note, your winged friend does not have to be the same sex as you—you can use a girl if you are a guy or a guy if you are a girl. The key here is to make sure that the vibe you give off is platonic—no flirting with your wingman, ladies! (And vice versa.) In fact, I am a huge fan of single guys using their friends that are girls as a wingwoman. It can give the guy automatic points, because women will subconsciously place him in the "good guy, he gets along with girls and probably isn't an asshole" territory. It can be very charmingly disarming to a woman when your friend who's a girl makes the introduction. It's a little trickier when a woman uses a guy as her wingman, though, as there tends to be an Alpha male syndrome where the other guys you want to flirt with may be put off by another man in the picture. It can work, though, if he has the ability to connect you with other guys, and step away. What's your wing-person's job exactly? We'll get to that shortly, when we talk about the plan.

Before we do that, let's just talk for a quick second about who to leave behind. There are certain people that you should never bring along if you are looking to get your flirt on, and you probably already know who I'm talking about. These are the people

---

Flirting Tip #7

Grab a fun and flirty wingman to increase your odds and guarantee a good time.

---

who are going to bring drama, try to steal the spotlight, will always get wasted, always be negative or somehow try to bring you down altogether. You can go out with these friends another time (if you really want to), but with those qualities, do you really want to? My friend Sarah had a wingwoman experience gone wrong. This is a story that I think will demonstrate how important your choices can be...

Sarah was ready to get back in the game. She'd had a nasty breakup a couple months past, and wanted to check out a singles mixer put on by a meetup.com group in her area. Giving little thought to it, Sarah asked her fun and flirty friend Megan to come with her. Sarah wanted a little extra support since it was her first night back out in the dating pool. The two women arrived at the event ready to mingle, and they hit the open bar. Problem was, Megan never left the bar. An hour into the event, she was wasted.

Sarah forged on nevertheless, and started talking to a nice guy we will call Bill. They hit it off—they had similar interests and they were definitely attracted to each other. Ten minutes in, and Megan decided to destroy their conversation. She started blatantly hitting on Bill herself and put herself physically in between Bill and Sarah. In an effort to avoid drama, and to get as far away from Megan as possible, Bill disappeared. Completely.

Sure, Bill might not have ended up being the right guy for Sarah, but who knows? She lost the opportunity to even find out, because of a terrible wingwoman. Don't lose an opportunity the way Sara did. Take the time to find someone who will cover you in the dogfight that we call dating.

Can't find a friend who can work for you? Too shy to ask for help? Don't have any friends that can hold back on taking that fifth shot of tequila for one night? Don't fear, there is another option. In the past few years there has been a surge of winged "professionals" on the market—people who you can pay to hang out with you for the night to help you out. Some seem legit and others appear to be closer to escorts (at least to me based on their sites), but the legit ones could be a fun. I have actually acted as a wingwoman for several of my clients. It shows them all that they are capable of, in action! Consider a professional only if you don't have a friend that fits the bill, but do your research first and check their reviews.

HAVE A PLAN, MAN.

An essential component of bringing on a wingman is *the plan*. Your wingman has a very specific role for the night, and it's important to figure all that out before you start flirting. It is essential to determine the 5 W's—Who, What, Where, When and Why:

- **Who**—Who are you looking to meet? Do you have a type for the night? Maybe you are looking for someone different from the kind of person you usually go for—let your wingman know. Are you open to anything and anyone? Your wingman needs to know who to look for, who to avoid, and when to save you.

- **What**—What is the signal to let your wingwoman know when you either need help, or need space? A signal will let your wingman know when to back off or when to swoop in and save you. Have a code. A touch of your nose when you want to be saved? A wink when you want to be left alone? Anything can give a nonverbal cue for what you need your wingman to do.

- **Where**—Where are you planning on going? A bar or two? An event? Don't run mindlessly around the city, but have an idea of where your combined talents can best be used.

- **When**—When are you moving onto the next location? When do you want to wrap it up for the evening? I recommend hitting at least two locations with your wingwoman—remember, dating is a numbers game! So plan it out, map it out, and time it out. Have a rally location in case you separate, and set a time to meet there.

- **Why**—Why do you need your wingwoman? Is it to break the ice? To start a conversation and then quietly step away? Or is it to make sure you don't get too drunk, have food in your teeth, or laugh too loud? Let your partner-in-crime know just what you need from her.

A good plan will lead to a great night. I have always said that the cause of all frustrations is expectations, so if you and your wingwoman both keep your expectations in check, and you have a plan that spells out your *modus operandi* (you may have heard of an M.O.—and that's what it stands for) for the night, you will be set for a super fun experience! Oh—don't forget to appreciate your winged friend. Buy her (or him) a couple drinks, say thank you—a great wing-person is priceless!

GET FEARLESS

- Find a fun and flirty friend to be your wingman or wing-woman—just make sure they meet the criteria!
- Make a plan and set expectations to ensure a great night.

4

Safety First

"Precaution is better than cure."
-Edward Coke

Not so fast there! Before I give you the steps to becoming an opposite-sex magnet, I need to make sure that you are prepared in terms of safety. Flirting can be a VERY powerful tool, and you need to know how to handle situations where your super flirt skills may get you more than you bargained for. It happens! You may be at the bar, see someone you like from afar, use the tips in the next chapter, and then BAM—you are in a full-fledged flirty conversation. Next thing you know this new person is inviting you to dinner, out for more drinks, or trying to make out with you at the bar. If you're still interested after your conversation, great! Plan a date and see where it goes. If not, you need to learn how to shut the flirtation down so that no one gets the wrong idea.

There are some safety rules you have to follow to make sure you're always in control of the situation. It just wouldn't be right to unleash you into the world with so much power and no way to control it. So without further ado, you should know that safety in flirting comes down to five rules:

- Lay Off the Sauce
- Make Sure You Have an ON/OFF Button
- Use the Buddy System
- Keep Your Privates Private
- Listen to YOU

Guys, make no mistake: these rules apply to you as well. Men are taken advantage of a lot more than you would think. So if you do not want to wake up with regrets (or a missing wallet), pay attention.

LAY OFF THE SAUCE

"First you take a drink, then the drink takes a drink, then the drink takes you." -F. Scott Fitzgerald

---

Alcohol is the greatest social lubricant in the world. It loosens you up and can turn some of the least confident introverts into people who dance on the bar and take body shots. Really. I've seen it. Humorous, but neither attractive or safe. I will never tell you not to drink while flirting. That would be insanely hypocritical as I do enjoy a beverage or two when I am out and about socializing. However, you need to stay within your limits.

It doesn't matter if you are driving or not—you need to keep yourself in check. Alcohol and its effects on your body are actually dictated by science—there is a chemical reaction that goes on between your brain, your body, and the booze. Understanding how it works is kind of important for any adult who enjoys imbibing now and then.

There are several online resources that can help you understand how alcohol affects your body. A great site to check out is www.brad21.org—*Be Responsible About Drinking*. The site has a chart that shows how alcohol impacts your ability to function, based on your weight and number of drinks. It also differentiates between men and women, because we metabolize alcohol differently. That chart (and most others online) will show you how many drinks you can have safely, and when you will probably be over the edge and should give your car keys to a designated driver. It's also pretty safe to say that if you shouldn't be driving, you shouldn't be flirting.

Not looking to get all technical? A good rule of thumb is to have one or two drinks and call it quits. If you need something to hold on to while you're out, order a club soda—no one needs to know that there isn't any vodka in it.

Flirting Tip #8

A martini or two is great, but three or four and you are in the danger zone. Keep it under control. Always.

The important thing to remember is that alcohol is not evil. It has a place, in moderation. My concern is that if you are three sheets to the wind, and manage to remember the flirting tips in this book despite your inebriated state, you might not be able to decipher whether you are flirting with friend or foe. Flirting while drunk can get you in trouble. Play it safe and stay off the sauce…for the most part.

GET FEARLESS

- Enjoy alcohol as the social lubricant that it can be, BUT
- Know your limits.
- If you *don't* know your limits, *don't drink*. Period.

MAKE SURE YOU HAVE AN ON/OFF BUTTON

"I'm not afraid of storms, for I'm learning to sail my ship." -Louisa May Alcott

---

Don't worry, we aren't turning into bots, but there are a few main controls that we need to make sure are installed in our brains to stay in control during flirtatious encounters. One of the most important when it comes to flirting is the ON/OFF button. Your use of that button is a super-important skill when you are flirting and start to feel uncomfortable. Is the person you are flirting with getting the wrong idea and coming on too strong? Are they taking your conversation past the boundaries of your comfort zone? Are you not interested in them romantically (whether you never were, or changed your mind), but they seem to be on an entirely different page? If any of these apply, it is time to turn it OFF.

My friend Kim has had this happen multiple times. She probably has enough expertise to be my co-author on this book—she is an amazing flirt! Kim is charismatic and really knows how to work the room. She engages people in conversation and can make anyone feel like the center of the universe. The problem is that sometimes she doesn't know when to scale it back. There have been at least a few times when she was merely being fun, flirty and nice, and it was taken as an invitation for much more. Do you know what is more awkward than someone you are not interested in trying to kiss you? And then you dodge their lips like there's a bullet coming your way? Nothing. Nothing is more awkward.

There are telltale signs that can help you see if someone is getting the wrong idea (or too much of the right idea). These signs include:

- They become a little too touchy-feely—grazing your shoulder is okay, but knee rubbing? Not so much.
- They start talking super-close to your face.
- The conversation turns entirely to sex.
- They try to get you to leave wherever you are to see their "amazing apartment."

I am not here to judge, so if any of the above "wrong idea" categories are okay with you, I won't hold it against you. (Although I have to take a stand and say that I would never ever endorse going the apartment/house/boat/car of someone you just met at a bar. Especially if you have exceeded your drink limits. It is just not smart, and if they are genuinely interested, there will be plenty of time for that a couple [or several] dates down the road.)

In general, if you see any of the above signs and aren't feeling it, it is time to turn your flirting switch from ON to OFF. Just how do you do that? Well, you work in reverse. The last thing you want to do is embarrass or offend, but a few anti-flirt moves can do the trick to let your conversation partner know it just isn't going to happen:

- **Space it out**—Create more physical space between the two of you. Move your chair back or take a step away. A physical barrier is the best way to put the brakes on intimacy.

- **Eliminate touch**—There are people who are naturally "touchy," but as you will learn (if you don't already know!), touch can send signals to the other person that you are interested. Take touch out of the equation so there are no mixed messages. Even a platonic pat on the back can be misinterpreted once the line has been crossed, so keep your hands at your sides.

- **Redirect the conversation**—Stay away from anything related to sex. Period. Talk about the weather. There is nothing less sexy than the weather.

- **Run!**—Okay, maybe not run, but excuse yourself and exit the situation completely. Make up a reason if necessary—feign illness, say you need to go to the bathroom, say that you have to get up early the next day, or go make a phone call. Just find a reason to leave.

A simple redirection can make all the difference between being in a completely uncomfortable situation and your comfort zone. There is never a reason to be rude, but it is essential to stay in control.

GET FEARLESS

- Locate your on/off button.
- Use the anti-flirt techniques to pull back a conversation that has gone over the edge.

USE THE BUDDY SYSTEM

"In a friend you find a second self." - Isabelle Norton

In chapter 3 we talked all about the people you should bring with you to help you flirt, to help you meet people, and to support you in your search for Mr. or Ms. Right. This section is all about the buddy system for a different reason. It's about surrounding yourself with people who will keep you safe. Maybe you went a little overboard and drank a few more than your limit of martinis? Maybe you're not as comfortable walking away from a situation where someone is becoming a little too receptive to your flirting techniques? That's where your buddy comes in. Having a buddy can mean the difference between a regretful morning-after, or an even scarier encounter. This buddy doesn't have to be a super flirt; they just have to care about your wellbeing.

Your buddy needs to know the signals of when to swoop in and help you get out of a situation that makes you uncomfortable. I make a habit of surrounding myself with people who know my personality, and can read when I look like I want out of a situation. If you're heading out in your hometown, try to bring along a friend or two who has those same talents. Even if they can't read you like a book, just having a friend with you is very important. At the very least, it will give you someone to drag into the conversation or provide you with an excuse to exit—"My friend is looking lonely, I better go hang out with her! Nice to talk to you!" Your friends really do make great excuses available to you.

What if a buddy is simply not available? That happens, I know. In chapter 2 we went through a ton of places to meet people, and some of those places are going to be locations where you're generally going to be by yourself. Hotel bars, airports, parks—many times you are going to be flirting at these locations alone. You won't have your group of girl friends or guy friends around to swoop in when you're not comfortable.

If a buddy is completely unavailable, and you are looking to flirt and meet people, you need to be even more cautious and

---

Flirting Tip #9

Bring a friend, not just as a wingman or wingwoman, but to keep you from uncomfortable situations.

---

abide by all the rest of the safety rules in this chapter—especially the rules applying to alcohol! So if you do decide to hit up the hotel bar and flirt with the sexy stranger sitting on the stool next to you, just make sure that you stay in control of the situation. Remember all of the other tips in this chapter urging you to stay in control. Simply having someone with you, or being smart about your surroundings, can keep you safe.

GET FEARLESS

- Always bring a flirting buddy with you if possible.
- If you don't have a buddy, it is that much more important to stay in check and under control.

KEEP YOUR PRIVATES PRIVATE

"Privacy is not something that I'm merely entitled to, it's an absolute prerequisite." - Marlon Brando

---

Get your mind out of the gutter—not *those* privates! The "privates" I am focused on here is all of your personal information.

You are going to meet people in many different locations, and most of those people don't need to know *that* much about you—including your full name, your phone number, your address, where you work, where you live, where you play, where your kids play, etc. This is all information that you need to keep close to the vest for at least the first couple of encounters.

I am not saying that you have to act as if you're in the CIA and on a super-secret mission, but providing personal information in this day and age can be dangerous. The person you're meeting in a bar is likely a complete stranger you know nothing about. I don't want to make you paranoid or scared of going out there and meeting people, but the sad fact of the matter is that there are people out there who do not have the best of intentions. If you live alone or you're a single parent, it becomes that much more dangerous to give out your personal info.

Think about what someone could find out with just the little amount of information you give them. If you give someone a business card, they could know a tremendous amount about you with a simple Google search. They'll have your first and last name, where you work, and the city you work in. Take what happened to Rob as an example…

Rob is 32, single, and a total catch. He is constantly dating, but just hasn't met someone he wants to settle down with. He is a fantastic conversationalist, and on his way home from work one day he found himself chatting up a beautiful woman on the train. Their short conversation came to an abrupt stop when he arrived at his destination, but because he was interested, he flipped Isabel his business card and asked her to email him.

By the time Rob got back to his apartment (just 10 minutes from the train station), he had a friend request on Facebook, a LinkedIn request, and an email from Isabel. Taken aback at her unexpected (and somewhat unseemly) eagerness, Rob decided to ignore her for the night and respond in the morning to her email. However, when Rob arrived in the office the following morning he had 3 messages on his voicemail from Isabel wondering why he was so rude, and she threatened to come to his office and ask him in person. Yikes!

Use your business cards for business purposes only, or you will never know who is going to show up at your cubicle wondering why you didn't call them back. This is actually one of the reasons I developed FlipMe.com—to protect women's personal information until they felt more comfortable and to offer an alternative to providing a business card. Giving out all of that information can be a mistake; hedge your bets and keep it to yourself.

So when you are out and about meeting people, you need to keep the information you disseminate to a minimum, at first. After a couple of dates (or a background check), do what you will—but until then keep your personal information personal. Here are some good tips for protecting your privates:

Flirting Tip #10

Only share your first name with people you've just met. Use a "dating email" address until you know them.

- Give out your first name only.

- Do not talk about where you live in specifics—if you tell to someone you live in New York City, it's going take them a long time to find you given that NYC includes five boroughs and millions of people. However if you say "I live on 80th and Third," there is a far greater chance of this stranger showing up at your neighborhood coffee shop looking for you.

- If you give out an e-mail address, have a dating e-mail address set up through Gmail or Hotmail account. A dating email address doesn't have your name in the address itself, and doesn't have your full name as the display name—it is completely generic, e.g., nycguy@ or funchick@. Also, make sure that it is not linked to your Facebook or Twitter account. Both of those sites allow you to find friends via an email address, and if you provide the email attached to Facebook or Twitter, anyone can find you.

- If you give out a phone number, make sure it's your cell number. Most cell phones are untraceable except as far as the general location where the service provider is located. In contrast, if you have a landline, it can often be reverse-searched to find your address.

In short, keep all personal information that can make you easily identifiable to a minimum. Once you get to know each other better and you realize that this new person wasn't just released from the state penitentiary, feel free to invite him or her over for a coffee! Until then, take care of yourself. You may think I'm going a little overboard with this advice, but I've been witness to *a lot* of sticky situations. The best-case scenario is to be cautious and then to let your guard down slowly—because it's a lot harder to clean up a mess after the fact.

GET FEARLESS

- Keep your personal information to yourself.
- Set up a "dating" email address with Gmail or Hotmail.
- Give your business card out for business purposes only.

LISTEN TO YOU

"Don't try to comprehend with your mind. Your minds are very limited. Use your intuition." - Madeleine L'Engle, A Wrinkle in Time

This world is filled with noise. The people around you will talk *to* you, talk *at* you and try to fill you with *their* opinions. In all areas of life, you need to listen to an element inside of you called intuition, otherwise known as your gut. Your intuition is especially important in the realm of flirting and dating—and can help keep you safe.

You've been provided with an ability to assess situations, an ability that you might not even know exists. Everyone has intuition. That feeling in your stomach that you get when something doesn't feel right? That's real. That is your brain saying to you that something just isn't kosher. It is not just your imagination. So if you are out getting your flirt on, and you get that feeling in your stomach that something isn't right—it probably isn't. Consider that a cue that you need to step away. No one else is going to be able to read a situation like you will, and no one else will have the same reaction to certain circumstances that you will—so you need to listen to yourself. Your friends might be saying, "She is hot! Go for it!" or "What are you, crazy? That guy is perfect for you." But if you are feeling uncomfortable, it is only *your* opinion that matters.

Often it's difficult to hear your inner self when everything else around you is so loud and distracting. Sometimes you have to do a little work to hear more clearly what you have to say, to you. So let's focus on developing that inner self. There are many ways to get in touch with your intuition, and it's worth a little effort to tune in. Meditation and yoga are great ways to start—focusing on yourself and your thoughts instead of letting the rest of the world in can help you get more in tune. Try a yoga class just once, and you'll be surprised how you feel after spending an hour on you. Just recognizing that your intuition exists and acknowledging its usefulness will help build your intuition. Awareness and openness can be very powerful. There are hundreds of books, YouTube videos and online articles that can help you with exercises to tap into your intuition. Some require a more open mind than others, and can seem a little "new age," but don't be shy to try—many are extremely effective.

Flirting Tip #11

Trust your gut! Intuition can be an amazing resource to both find who to flirt with, and who to run from.

Regardless of what you do to embrace this inner friend, getting in tune with and listening to your intuition is probably one of the greatest safety mechanisms that I can recommend in relation to keeping yourself safe while dating. If you are ever in a situation that your gut is telling you isn't right, listen to yourself and get the hell out.

GET FEARLESS

- Recognize that you have an intuitive ability.
- Take the time to tune into that intuition through meditation or other exercises.
- Pay attention to your gut when you are out socializing.

5
The Five Steps to Becoming a Super Flirt

"Flirting is the gentle art of making a man feel pleased with himself." -Helen Rowland

Y ou are ready! You are now prepared mentally, your confidence is boosted, your attitude is right, your location selected, your wingman is on tap, and your safety checks are in place. It's now time to become a super flirt! Becoming a super flirt is not as hard as you may think; sometimes it just takes a little practice A few extra smiles won't hurt! Being engaging and nice can be fun—promise.

There are people who are just naturally charismatic and flirtatious, and there are some people who have to work at it. There is absolutely nothing wrong with having to put a little effort forward to become the flirt that you'll see you were born to be. Once you have mastered the art of flirtation, you will be able to take over the world…or at least, connect with people. Either is helpful in achieving your dreams.

You might think that some of these tips are clichéd, repetitive, or basic. However, I've found out through repeated practice (mine, and others') that these are the tips that work the best and produce results. Moreover, these tips concern the things that people *forget* to do. Sometimes you just have to be reminded of what you already know, and sometimes you need to be taught new things. Regardless of where you fall in that scale, you will make better connections and meet more people when using the information I am about to lay out for you.

Well! Let's get to it! This chapter lays out the five core techniques for becoming a successful flirt, and they are:

1. Smiles

2. Eye contact

3. Good conversation

4. Body language

5. Touch

Seems pretty simple, right? Combine all of these elements and you will be unstoppable! Let's break each one down, and make you a flirting machine. So get on up!

1. SAY CHEESE—THE IMPORTANCE OF A SMILE

"Every time you smile at someone, it is an action of love, a gift to that person, a beautiful thing." - Mother Teresa

---

The first rule of flirting is to put a smile on your face. Seems simple, right? Well it is, but there's nothing wrong with doing something simple—especially when it *works*. A smile changes EVERYTHING about you. What you say, how you say it, and how your words are perceived are completely changed when you're speaking with a smile. You can literally insult someone to their face (not recommended, FYI), but if it is said with a smile you have given yourself at least a 10-second head start to run before they realize what you really said (and try to clock you).

Your smile is the first go-to when you're trying to flirt with someone. Do you know that studies have shown that most people decide within THREE SECONDS whether or not they find you attractive? Your smile can change everything, and make you that much more appealing. Seriously, research has shown that a smile actually increases your attractiveness—a semi-attractive person who's smiling will actually be perceived as better looking than a not-smiling attractive person.

Try it out for a while. Maybe you aren't the chipperest of people, but simply try showing those pearly whites a little more often. Did you know that smiling actually *causes* happiness? Yup, when you smile, it sends little signals to your brain that makes you think you are happy. Talk about faking it until you make it! So start smiling, even if for no reason at all. You may be surprised how your attitude changes, and how the attitudes of others change in response to you. Meet one of my clients, Sue…

> *Sue was a very happy person but hated to smile. Everyone who knew her thought she had a great smile, but she was so self-conscious about the way her eyes crinkled that she almost never truly smiled (or laughed, for that matter). She had perfected the art of the closed-mouth smile. You know, the one that looks like a constipated smirk? She came to me because despite being attractive she had a very difficult time meeting men either online or off. It was easy to see why! Who is looking through Match.com pictures for someone who looks like they need a laxative? Sue's in-person "smile" was the same and was the reason that she wasn't being approached at events or bars.*
>
> *After an in-the-field experiment where smiley, crinkly-eyed Sue was unleashed, her world changed. All because of her real smile. She came to terms with her crinkliness, and learned that no one cared about it but her! In fact, it was*

cute and endearing. Why? Because it was genuine, authentic and made her look as happy on the outside as she is on the inside. After revamping her online dating profile photos and smiling every chance she gets in the real world, I am happy to say Sue is getting contacted and approached more than ever. Now her biggest challenge is weeding through her prospects.

Your smile is an essential addition to your flirting repertoire. The bigger the better, and the brighter the better, too. I have to take a minute here in honor of my dentist who, combined with my parents, made me a complete stickler for clean, bright teeth and oral hygiene. I would be a terrible person if I had you flashing your gums without a little prep work. Smiles filled with white, beautiful teeth are simply phenomenal. Don't have perfectly aligned teeth? Don't sweat it. Jewel seemed to make it work for her, with other greats like Lauren Hutton. However, dirty nasty yellow teeth are

---

Flirting Tip #12

Everything starts with a smile. It changes the way people see you, and the way that you speak and feel.

---

never flirty and hot. Smoking and drinking tea or coffee can do a number on your teeth. Take a moment to get your teeth bleached, either professionally, or using an over-the-counter process like Crest Whitestrips. It can make a world of difference.

Okay. PSA over, but the moral of the story is: flash those pearly whites often (after making sure they are in the best possible condition). In conversation with someone you want to flirt with? Remind yourself to smile. See someone you like from across the room? Smile. Don't see a soul you want to talk to? Smile anyway—it will make you feel good. Now get out there, and go get 'em, tiger!

GET FEARLESS

- Force yourself to smile—at everyone.
- Make it a full smile, crinkly eyes and all.
- For a week make a list of everything that genuinely brings a full-on smile to your face. Keep those moments in mind when you need a pick-me-up!

2. BAT THOSE EYES—WHY EYE CONTACT IS KEY

"Almost nothing need be said when you have eyes."
- Tarjei Vesaas, The Boat in the Evening

They say the eyes have it. I'm not sure who "they" are, but "they" are right. Your eyes speak VOLUMES louder than anything coming out of your mouth—especially when flirting. It almost makes up for not saying anything, or saying the wrong thing. Eye contact is where it's at. There are two ways that eye contact is used in flirting: first, to attract the initial approach or subconscious invite, and second, during conversation. Each is very important to starting and keeping a connection going.

Initial Contact

Initial eye contact is intended to either encourage someone to approach you (typically the woman does the encouraging), or to determine if someone would be receptive to an approach (typically the guy is the one who checks this out). It's all about that very first connection, and eye contact is probably one of the most important aspects of the flirt that you will ever do. Proper eye contact for the initial flirt has two rules:

1. Eye contact must be accompanied by a smile.

2. Eye contact cannot be held for too long or too short a period of time.

We just talked all about how your smile is an essential tool in the arsenal of the art of flirting, so adding a smile to eye contact is like a one-two punch. Sure you can do one without the other, but the combo is how you take 'em down. Figuring out how long to hold that eye contact is a little trickier.

Timing proper eye contact can take some practice. The standard should be somewhere around 3 seconds. Any less and your eye contact can easily be mistaken for a passing glance. Any more than three seconds and the object of your affection might contact the authorities. Even 3 seconds seems pretty long in practice, but it works. Those three seconds let the person know that you are looking at them on purpose... deliberately... that it isn't a mistake. It is almost a 100% guarantee that if you direct this three-second eye contact at a man, he will approach. If you are a guy looking to test this out, you need to look for a return smile. That is your key to the city. See a smile? Go on over there and introduce yourself!

Use the building blocks of a smile and eye contact and you are on your way to becoming a wo/man magnet!

GET FEARLESS

- Spot someone you are attracted to, put yourself in their line of sight (no more than 10 feet away if possible) and make eye contact. You can work from farther distances, but if there are people in the way it can get confusing for the object of your eye affections.

- While making eye contact, smile and hold for 3 seconds. Look for a returned smile—got one? Wait for the approach—or make it yourself! More on that later...

During Conversation

Just because you make eye contact to get that initial approach (or invitation to approach) doesn't mean you can stop there. Once you are actually holding a conversation with the object of your intentions, your eye contact has to continue. Don't start looking away during the conversation with that person you roped in with those beautiful browns—you have got to keep it up. Your eyes will tell the story, along with your words and body language. When you're speaking with someone (anyone), the golden rule says you should try and maintain as much eye contact as you feel comfortable with. Some people are more comfortable than others when it comes to this, and it's one of those things that can take a lot of practice. You *can* get better at it and become more comfortable in making consistent eye contact. It's very worthwhile, since this practice will benefit you far beyond flirting and dating. There have been many studies done that indicate that a person's perceived trustworthiness is dependent on how much eye contact they have with others. People who shift their eyes too often, look down, or simply don't engage as much as the average person may be seen as less trustworthy. I know you are amazing, and dependable and honorable, and you do not want to misrepresent yourself by failing to make enough eye contact.

The *type* of eye contact you make is equally as important. You may not realize it, but you speak with your eyes more than you know. There are small movements and reflexes that happen subconsciously in your eyes depending on what you're thinking about. Recognizing that your thoughts are reflected in your eyes, and using that knowledge to your advantage when flirting is an amaz-

---

Flirting Tip #13

Use eye contact to let someone know you are interested and listening to what they say.

---

ing technique. Righ now, take a minute and pull out a mirror. Look yourself in the eyes and think of the saddest possible thing you can imagine. Your dog dying, starving children, or anything that is horribly depressing. Take a look at the way your eyes react to those thoughts. Then think of happy things, like a hot first date, lots of money in the bank, a new car! Look at the way your eyes react. Do you see the difference? It might not be a massive change in your appearance, but there are minor changes in the direction, shape and brightness of your eyes depending on your thoughts.

Now, how can you use that to your advantage? You are going to think amazing happy thoughts when you are flirting. You're going to look at the person you're flirting with and think that they are the most amazing person in the world. Look at them like they are the best thing since sliced bread. They might not be, and you may never speak to them again, but you are going to pretend for that moment that they're fantastic. It will show in your eyes and it will come off as positivity being reflected through your eye contact to the person that you're flirting with. Just like with a smile, it can change everything that they perceive about you. It's all about the power of positive thinking. Who knows—maybe they are amazing! And using these practices, you'll definitely get a chance to find out!

GET FEARLESS

- Maintain eye contact as much as possible during conversations.

- Go for that extra sparkle, and think happy thoughts while you're flirting.

3. CHATTY CATHY—START A CONVERSATION AND KEEP IT GOING

"Conversation. What is it? A Mystery! It's the art of never seeming bored, of touching everything with interest, of pleasing with trifles, of being fascinating with nothing at all." - Guy de Maupassant

You cannot talk about flirting without talking about talking. The art of conversation is one of the biggest challenges for most flirters or daters in general. *What do I talk about? How can I change the direction of a boring conversation? Why do I feel stupid talking about myself? Do I have to start with the weather?* It's one of the most nerve-racking aspects of flirting—likely because it is clearly one of the most important. If you cannot have a good conversation, all of the eye contact and smiling in the world won't save you. People are looking for connections, and connections involve communication, and communication involves conversation. Don't fret, though: the art of holding a good conversation can be learned.

A good flirty conversation involves three elements—I call it giving good LIP:

- Lighten Up
- Listen In
- Keep it Positive

Lighten Up

"Fun is good." -Dr. Seuss

There are a lot of super-smart people in this world. They are everywhere looking to talk about smart things, debate theories, and consider the world's weighty topics. I am sure their IQs far exceed mine, but I'll tell you something I know that they might not—there is absolutely *no place* for that kind of conversation in an initial flirtation, or during the first few dates. When you first meet someone they are looking to connect with you superficially (but with a promise of depth). Now to be clear, by "superficially" I do not mean your looks, but rather, they are looking to keep things at the surface and not to scratch too deep right away. They do want the *promise* of depth, just not right away. Serious conversations that have the possibility of polarizing a couple should be saved for when you actually are a couple, not during a first encounter. So keep it light and fluffy—nothing but the proverbial puppies and rainbows!

The following topics NEVER belong in an initial conversation:
- religion
- politics
- babies
- marriage
- medications
- therapy
- crazy exes

Flirting and the conversation that accompanies it have to be FUN! There is nothing fun about your crazy ex-boyfriend who no longer takes his antipsychotics and sometimes pops by your apartment unannounced. You think I'm kidding, but Stacy told that story during an initial conversation. The guy listened to it and never came back from the bathroom. Stacy was so clueless that she actually wondered why. Well, she wondered why until she told me the story, and I flicked her in the forehead. She now saves that tidbit until a couple of dates in, but her dates know her a little better by that point and think twice before running for the hills. She is only a restraining order away from not telling the story at all.

Likewise, any conversations about heavy, debatable topics need to be saved for the third+ date. You just met this person, for goodness sake. You can wait a few dates to find out if he is a left-wing Buddhist like you or if she is willing to be a baby mama for your five kids-to-be.

Even outside of these "stay the hell away from" topics, there always needs to be an overall lightness to your flirty chatting. It might sound counterintuitive, but it's best if you are actually prepared for light conversation, especially if you are the type of person to go right into philosophical dialogue or if you get nervous when even thinking about talking to someone you find attractive. To prevent this, always have 2 or 3 topics of conversation that you can go to. Some of these include:

- restaurants in the area you tried recently
- an upcoming event or concert that you're going to
- a recent trip you took
- the freaking weather

Yes, I said talk about the weather. If it's a choice between debating Plato's teachings and talking about the chance of rain the next day, always go with the rain.

The point of keeping it light is to keep the conversation flowing and prevent people from either clamming up or clenching their fists. After all, the point of an initial flirt is to show off your personality and to see if you two want to talk again. Once you're on a date you can delve a little bit deeper (still not too far at first), but it's all about the build-up until that point.

Here's a list of questions that will always get them talking:
- Where are you from?
- Have you been to any good restaurants around here lately?
- Have you seen any good concerts lately?
- What was the last movie you saw?
- What do you like to do when you aren't working?
- Where are your favorite places to travel?
- If you could live anywhere in the world, where would that be?

Flirting Tip #14

Always have something to talk about, and make sure that it's positive. Have 2 or 3 light topics always ready.

- What is the craziest thing you have ever done?
- What is your idea of a perfect date?
- When you were little, what did you want to be when you grew up?
- What is your dream job now?
- If you could eat one food for the rest of your life, what would it be?

- If you could invite any six people living or dead to dinner, who would they be?
- What was your first job?

All of these questions start a conversation and keep it going. It shows you are interested in hearing what they have to say, but the topics are light and fun. Conversely, there are certain questions you should never ask when you've just met. These include:

- Why are you single?
- How old are you? (Which should never be followed up with, "No! Really, how old are you?")
- Why did your last relationship fail?
- Describe your perfect wife/husband.
- How many kids do you want?
- Are you into threesomes?

The list of what not to ask could go on forever. It doesn't matter what you say, as long as you keep it light and avoid fighting words.

Don't forget to use humor—if you're funny. Humor can be HOT! However, if you are not funny, it can be the death sentence to a conversation. If you are funny and can come up with quick and witty responses, go for it! Your sex appeal will go through the roof (if the object of your affection has a sense of humor). If you are not so funny (but think you are) or if your counterpart lacks a humor gene, it is just not going to mesh well. So my advice here? Be funny…if you can.

GET FEARLESS

- Keep your conversations light.
- Have 2 or 3 go-to topics to talk about in case you get nervous.
- Avoid the "stay the hell away from" list.

Listen In

"The greatest compliment that was ever paid me was when one asked me what I thought, and attended to my answer." - Henry David Thoreau

---

"Oh, enough about me! Say, what do *you* think of me?" We all have been in one-sided conversations. How fun are they, right? Not so much. That's why you are going to be the greatest conversationalist ever, by saying nothing. Okay, maybe not nothing, but you surely aren't going to be dominating the conversation. You are going to focus on being a good listener. Being a good listener is essential in flirting and dating—it shows that you are paying attention, and paying attention to them shows that you like them. If it sounds like we are back in kindergarten, well ... we kind of are. These are skills we learned long ago, but may have lost along the way.

Follow these five steps and you will be a superstar listener:

1. **Eliminate distractions.** This is a biggie! We are so addicted to our cell phones that the thought of not having your iPhone ready and waiting to let us know when Bob, Aunt Sue or Best Buy is contacting you is almost painful. However, if you really want to be a good listener, keep the cell phone on silent and out of sight. Avoid getting sucked into other distractions around you as well, like the TV above the bar, the fighting couple 10 feet away, or anything else that causes your mind and attention to wander. Paying attention can take some

effort, but the people you communicate with will infinitely appreciate it.

2. **Maintain eye contact.** Maintaining eye contact during your conversation is essential to let them know that you are actively listening. There is nothing worse than talking to someone who is looking everywhere but at you. So keep your eyes connected as they are speaking. Trust me, they will notice.

3. **Don't interrupt.** Sometimes you may have a burning desire to interject your opinions or experiences while people are talking. Interrupting can be a cultural, regional or innate trait. Trust me, I have met many people in New York that just cannot seem to keep their opinions to themselves for more than a second. However, if your goal is to be a good listener, it is extremely important that you do not interrupt. Let them speak it out. Let them tell their story (even if it's painfully long). Let them talk about something that you don't agree with, and just listen. Keep your opinions to yourself for now. There will be plenty of time to debate, interject your own position, or tell a similar story later on. Right now it is all about them, and trust me—they will love it.

4. **Encourage by offering meaningful follow-up questions.** Being an active listener requires speaking. Just a little bit, when you ask meaningful follow-up questions. Take their content and turn it into questions that extend the conversation. For example, say Steve is telling Tricia about a recent trip to Italy. Tricia can ask Steve about what his

favorite city was. After Steve tells her all about that city, she can ask about his favorite meal on the trip. That favorite meal question can transition into asking about his favorite foods in general. It's an endless cycle of content and follow-up. You are asking questions that show that you're paying attention—instead of just jumping from subject to subject because you've zoned out.

5. **Use your body.** There are certain things that you can do through body language that will subconsciously deliver the message that you are being an active listener. A few ways to use body language to show you're listening:

Flirting Tip #15

Active listening is a key to flirtation. Pay attention to what your date has to say and ask follow-up questions.

- **Relax**—Have a relaxed body expression. Don't tense up and look like you are ready to pounce. Research has shown that leaning forward with a relaxed posture demonstrates your interest.
- **Make faces**—Your facial expression should also show that you're listening. Match your facial expression to what they are saying. If they are telling a happy story, smile; if they are telling a sad story, look sad. Your facial expression can give away much of what is actually going on in your head, and should be focused on reflecting how good of a listener you are.

- **Move your head**—Nod your head when appropriate to let them know that you're in agreement.
- **Remain open**—Keep your posture open and inviting. Don't fold your arms across your chest. Face towards them and keep your upper body directed at them.

All of these are ways to show someone that you're listening. Using these techniques will make them feel your focus, and in turn make them feel like the center of the universe, at least for that moment. So listen up; the object of your affection will love your attention.

GET FEARLESS

- Recognize that everyone loves to have an attentive audience.
- Use the tips to focus on them. Sit back and enjoy listening (or at least try to… and if necessary, pretend).

Keep it Positive

A good flirtatious conversation has to be 100% positive. Along with confidence, positivity is one of the most attractive qualities. Positive people are magnetic. Essentially, everyone wants to feel good and be happy. So when you are having an initial conversation with someone, it needs to be as close to sunshine and roses as possible. We have spent a lot of time talking about the power of positivity and positive thinking, because it continues to come into play when you are becoming the super-flirt that you were born to be.

Compliments

Compliments are one of the greatest forms of positive communications that you will ever use—while flirting, or even just plain relating to someone. I have literally been complimenting people since I could speak. When asked how I became a flirting expert, my answer is always the same: I have been flirting since I was born. Part of that flirting has always been the art of the compliment. I was doing it before I even realized what I was doing. I vividly remember complimenting people on their clothing or their hair when I was only five years old, and receiving mystified but appreciative and positive reactions. It still works the same to this day, because underneath it all people are looking for acceptance and love—and giving compliments demonstrates that you have those qualities in abundance.

Genuine authentic compliments directed at the object of your affection will get you a better reception than almost any other effort. The key is to make sure that the flattery is genuinely meant. A generic or altogether canned compliment will not have the same

Flirting Tip #16

Flirting is about making someone feel good, and compliments are the easiest way to do that!

effect as something that you actually believe about that person. For example, if you think that they have gorgeous eyes, let them know it—just don't tell them in a way that makes it sound like a cheesy pick-up line. Say it authentically, such as, "I love listening to what you're saying, but I'm so distracted because you have the most gorgeous eyes I've ever seen." Depending on the conversation, there is a limitless supply of material. If someone told you a story about overcoming adversity or surmounting a challenge in their life, repay them with some kind words about their strength and perseverance. If they are talking about a great restaurant in the area that they frequent, compliment them on their exceptional taste. The possibilities for finding something that you can comment on and deliver praise about are endless.

In addition to starting a conversation, compliments continue the conversation. You can literally compliment anyone about anything, and as long as you mean it, it will work to raise their level of interest in you.

The spin

Beyond compliments, there are many other ways to keep the conversation positive, and that's especially important when you're talking about yourself. As mentioned previously, the goal in flirting is to focus on the other person—to make them feel good and to pay attention to what they are saying. However, you eventually have to talk too, and positivity is all about how you frame your answers.

You may have gone through a terrible divorce, struggled with disease or illness, or just had a tough run of it. However, when it comes to flirtation, especially in those initial conversations, you need to spin it in a positive light. So if you were recently divorced, don't talk about how terrible your ex-wife or ex-husband is. Talk about how you've been provided a second chance and you're enjoying connecting with new people in this fun and exciting stage of your life. If you just recovered from a serious illness such as cancer, talk about it, but talk about it as the survivor that you are and as the strong amazing person that you have become because of it. Maybe you've just had some bad luck lately. In initial conversations, all of the discussion needs to be focused on the positive aspects of life, so in spite of negative recent experiences, talk about how everything is turning around—because frankly, it could be—you just met someone new and exciting!

I am not in any way saying that you need to pretend to be someone else for the entirety of the relationship, but right now there is no relationship—yet. Right now you are complete strangers and only getting to know each other *on the surface*. The last thing you want to do is to eliminate yourself from the running because of negativity. A couple of dates down the line you can get a little deeper and talk about some of the problems that you've overcome. In general though, it is always better to look on the bright side and remain positive!

GET FEARLESS

- Focus on the positive in your conversation and avoid negative topics (or at least put a positive spin on them).

- Use the art of the compliment—frequently!

4. MOVING YOUR BODY

"What you do speaks so loud that I cannot hear what you say." - Ralph Waldo Emerson

Our nonverbal cues are just as important as our verbal messages. Don't you want to make sure that *what you aren't saying says the right thing?* Using your body to flirt is one of the most important steps in making a connection. There is a subliminal conversation going on between you and the people around you, and the right body language can help get your message across. So what is the right body language and what should you avoid? Well, I'm here to tell you, in chapter 7. For now, let's go through the main do's and don'ts of moving your body and save the heavy lifting for a few pages down.

Body Language Do's

DO face your partner in conversation.

DO lean forward slightly while talking.

DO keep your arms open and relaxed.

DO mirror what your companion is doing.

Just as there are *do's* for using your body language, there are equally as many (if not more!) *don'ts* to keep in mind. The *don'ts* are sometimes even more important as you may not even realize that you are sending the wrong message. So many opportunities are lost when people fail to realize what their bodies are saying. Here are my top ten don'ts of body language:

Don't cross your arms.

Don't slouch or slump.

Don't pay attention to your phone.

Don't tap your fingers.

Don't clench your fists.

Don't lean away.

Don't yawn.

Don't avoid eye contact.

Don't give the cold shoulder—or your back.

Don't fidget.

Any of these *don'ts* would scream loud and clear to the person you're with, "I am not interested," even if you are not saying a word. Some of us do the things on the *don't* list without even thinking, and without intending to send that negative message. Paying attention to the nonverbal messages that your body puts out there can ensure that you are sending the right message.

The entire purpose of using body language while flirting is to make an immediate subconscious connection with someone, without having to say a word. It's about making them comfortable and having them realize that you are interested. The next time you're flirting, take a moment to assess your body language. Take a look at the direction of your body, where your hands are, if your legs are crossed, etc. You may be surprised how much of it comes naturally, and it can become even more effective when you add a few conscious movements. Remember, actions speak louder than words.

GET FEARLESS

Flirting Tip #17

Use your body to make connections. Show that you are receptive and paying attention.

- Use your body language to show the object of your affection that you are interested—lean in, face them with your arms open, and mirror their movements.

- Avoid the top ten body language *don'ts* to prevent sending the wrong message.

5. BREAK THE TOUCH BARRIER

"Touch has a memory." - John Keats

Ahhhh … touch. It is one of the most important, but also one of the most improperly used techniques when it comes to flirting. Breaking through that physical barrier between two people is one of the most powerful things that you can do to let someone know that you are interested in them romantically. Having some sort of touch exchanged is almost a requirement, and if there is absolutely no physical contact—however slight—between the flirters, it can be a sign that there just isn't a connection. However, if touch is not used properly, or isn't received well, it can lead to an insanely awkward encounter. There are some serious rules that you need to understand before breaking that touch barrier. Just know that when used properly, touch can send your flirtations through the roof.

Here are the four touchstones of touching:

1. **Read the body language.** You need to assess the situation before putting your paws on anyone. The entirety of chapter 7 is dedicated to reading someone's body language to see if they're interested in you, and how to use yours to let someone know you like them. If you are the slightest bit apprehensive, read that chapter first before touching anyone. The last thing you want to do is to touch some-

body who doesn't want to be touched. Touching can be a very personal occurrence. Have you ever tried to hug someone and they slouched away? Tried to shake a hand and they recoiled? Kiss someone (even on the cheek) and they dodged you like Mike Tyson's fist? Getting rejected on a touch can be an awful feeling for you, and it can be just as awful making someone else feel uncomfortable.

2. **Determine the right location.** Location, location, location—important in real estate and so many other matters. In a way, we're talking about real estate here—and the estate is your body, and someone else's. When it comes to touch, whether you're talking about a stranger or a lover, location is extremely important—but the rules are different for each. At no point in a flirtation situation should you ever touch a person somewhere that you wouldn't touch your mother. That might sound gross in this context, but I hope it gets the point across. You would touch your mom's shoulder, you would touch her hand, or her arm, and maybe her leg or her knee. These are all places you can touch in a platonic manner, and that's exactly where you should be touching your flirtatious counterpart. No groping at the bar, please. The point isn't to try and cop a feel; the purpose is to break down the physical barrier to create the beginnings of intimacy. A shoulder is just fine.

3. **Keep it short and sweet.** We are not caressing, we are not massaging. We are letting our hand impact someone else's physical space for only a mere few seconds. Any-

thing longer than that and it will be unbelievably awkward or send the wrong signals (especially from a woman
to a man—story to follow!). Overtouching is a flirting sin,
and anything beyond "minimal" can be so far overboard
that you might not be able to salvage the situation.

4. **Look for a return touch before a retouch.** Before you
even consider touching again, you need to see if you are
getting a mirrored response. Are they touching you back?
Do not dream about touching more than once unless
you've been touched in return.

The touchstones are essential to understand before implement-
ing, as touch is both extremely effective, and often misinterpreted.
It's amazing what you can learn from observation. Take my client
Tonya for example:

*Tonya seemed absolutely perfect. She was young, beautiful,
charismatic, and intelligent. Why the hell was she coming
to me for coaching? She shouldn't have needed any of my
advice, I thought. Apparently she could meet tons of people
but never got asked out on real dates. Still stumped after
our initial conversations, I wanted to see her in action. I
engaged the power of observation and took her to the near-
est pub. I sat in the corner and I let her do her thing. Within
minutes of arriving she was approached by a good looking
guy, and that's when the enlightenment occurred. This girl
did not stop touching.*

*Tonya started the conversation by touching his shoulder.
Two seconds later she was touching his hand, a minute after*

that she's touching his knee, and eventually she went in for
the face. This was all within the first 10 minutes! All of a
sudden I understood why she had a lot of one-night stands,
and no relationships. She was giving the wrong impression
to everyone she was connecting with.

Touch can be extremely powerful and send amazing signals to the other person that you're connecting with, but it can also send the wrong signals if it's overused. Clearly Tonya was overusing her strokes, and once she realized how her actions were being perceived, she was able to take it down a notch.

Use touch to show that you are interested. Just touch in the appropriate places, and for a limited time only!

Imagine that scenario in reverse. A man who essentially started groping the object of his affection within seconds of meeting, when they're still strangers? The cops would likely be called before he could even buy her a drink. Overtouch can go one of two ways— either creep someone out or turn them on to the point of no return. Tonya was engaging with willing participants, but you could just as easily have a situation where the recipient is not amenable.

The moral of the story is to use the power of touch to unleash your super flirt, but just like all super powers, you must first understand how to use it and control it. Now go get frisky!

GET FEARLESS

- Use touch to send your flirtations soaring, but read the body language first.
- Keep it clean and keep it brief.

When you put all of these tips together, they form a master plan to get your flirt on. All of the five elements: smiling, eye contact,

---

Flirting Tip #18

Use touch to show that you are interested. Just touch in the appropriate places, and for a limited time only!

---

conversation, body language, and touch are essential to becoming a super flirt. Not sure you can do it? I promise that you can. Practice is key. Use every opportunity you have to implement some or all of the tips. The more you use them, the more likely they will all end up as second nature. You've got this. I have faith in you!

6

Ice Breaking

"The person who risks nothing, does nothing, has nothing, is nothing, and becomes nothing. He may avoid suffering and sorrow, but he simply cannot learn and feel and change and grow and love and live." - **Leo F. Buscaglia**

If you ask most singles what the scariest aspect of meeting new people is, they will likely say "the initial approach." Figuring out how to do it, when to do it, and what to say can paralyze a person with fear—so much fear that often the chance can pass right by. Think about how many opportunities have been missed because of fear to even just say *hi*. Missed connections occur every day, and the majority of the time it's because fear prevented someone from taking a chance. You owe it to yourself to seize every opportunity. That could have been the love of your life in line at Starbucks, and now you're left with finding her on Craigslist Missed Connections for your only chance at happiness. Okay, maybe it isn't that dramatic, but you are going to miss out on a lot if you sit back and wait for things to happen. It's time to move! It's time to get off the bench and get in the game!

If you can put all of foundational steps together successfully, the approach is going to be like a walk in the park. It is only scary because there is a fear of the unknown, for about five seconds. Once you start the conversation and use those five tips, it is all smooth sailing. Or perhaps you'll realize you aren't interested and walk away—but at least you will have tried!

The Pre-Approach

Before approaching anyone and breaking the ice, I suggest you look for eye contact and a smile, or at least eye contact. Simply walking up to someone and starting a conversation cold without receiving any indication that they might be interested isn't something I'd advise you to do. Haven't seen a signal yet? Get in their line of sight and flash those pearly whites again. Once you have a positive response, whether it's a nod or a smile or something else, it's time to swoop in. I had a friend named Gary who was afraid of nothing. He approached everyone he found even remotely attractive. He didn't wait for a signal; he just walked up and introduced himself. It worked for the most part, but I am pretty sure he scared the shit out of a lot of women. My advice? Don't be a Gary. Save yourself some pain and get the nonverbal invitation first through eye contact and a smile. It is not always going to be 100% accurate, and they might not always be receptive, but it is one hell of a hint.

What to Say

What you should say when you first approach someone is the subject of endless debate, and some serious fodder for comedians. However, "pick-up lines" are serious business! Entire books are written about pick-up lines, full weekend workshops are given on how to use them, and thousands of dollars are spent by singles searching out what the best lines are. I recommend against almost all of them, unless 1) you are funny—like Chelsea Handler funny, or 2) the line is "Hi."

I have never met anyone who could successfully pull off, "Can I take a picture of you, so I can show Santa just what I want for Christmas." It is just not possible, unless you are a comic and can deliver it like a joke. The majority of the time, even if you are trying to be funny, many lines can be perceived as creepy. "Hi, I've been undressing you with my eyes all night long, and think it's time to see if I'm right" is creepy no matter how hilarious you (think you) are. When the lines were written for the FlipMe cards, they had to be either sincere or make you laugh, but we broke them into categories so you could match your personality. Missing a funny bone? Stick with the sweet. Can pull off "Here's Hoping You Can Read"—pick up a sassy deck. There was a little more leeway since the cards were designed for women (and we tend to get away with much more—sorry, guys!), but they had to be light and fun. Similar to what's on the cards, anything you say to someone as an icebreaker has to be light.

Once you find something that works for you—run with it on repeat! Whether it is a technique like one of the five listed below, or a standard line: *if it isn't broke, don't fix it*. Just don't use it multiple times within range of anyone who has already heard it—it might not make the greatest first impression on your new focus if they just heard you say the same thing to the girl a couple feet away. I once met a man who told me he always used "Have you seen my cat?" to women he thought were attractive on the streets of New York. I didn't get it, but cat lovers were smitten and sucked in—at least, until they realized it was just a line. Try to find something that won't get you in trouble later, but will give you the perfect entry point to connect with the cutie at the park.

So if that book you just bought that gives you the top 100 pickup lines is barred, what do you say? There are plenty of ways to approach people and start a conversation; there are some that are simply better than others. Here are my top five tips for breaking the ice:

1. **Hi, my name is**_____. Seriously, just say "Hi." Walk up to someone and introduce yourself. This sounds almost ridiculous, doesn't it? But it works. You really do not need much more than that. It almost doesn't matter where you are. At the grocery store and making eye contact with that cute guy in produce? Smile and say hi. It is that simple.

2. **Pay a compliment.** Compliments are like verbal currency. They are accepted everywhere and can get you

a lot in return. If you are standing on line at Starbucks next to a woman who's wearing an amazing outfit or has gorgeous hair, compliment her. Make it genuine and authentic and it will not come off as a creepy pick-up line. Just don't sexualize the situation by telling a woman that she has great legs, or a guy that he has a nice butt. Those types of approaches might get you more than you bargained for. Simply find something that you find attractive about the person you want to meet, and don't be afraid to tell them.

3. **Use the environment**—Use anything around you to comment on and start the conversation. Is it hot out? Talk about it to the cutie waiting for the subway next to you. Is your cooking class instructor crazy? Make fun of the teacher with your attractive classmate. (Okay, maybe not the last one—we are trying to stay positive here). It's all about taking in and talking about everything around you. The sky is the limit! (You can actually talk about the sky!)

4. **Ask a question**—Asking a question is one of the easiest ways to start a conversation. It could be about almost anything. Are you still on line at Starbucks? Asking "Is this place ever not busy?" or "Have you tried that new Coolatta?" It almost doesn't matter what the question is as long as it's lighthearted, fits into the situation, and is non-threatening. It will start the conversation that you're looking for.

5. **Ask for help**—Asking for help is one of my all-time favorite ways of starting a conversation with someone.

People naturally want to help each other, so much so that it's almost instinctual (well, at least for most). So if you need a little assistance from the cute guy at your favorite take-out joint to open the doors as you are walking out, ask him! Would you appreciate some assistance adjusting your bicycle seat from that cute bike girl chugging water a few feet away? Ask her! It's a beautiful thing.

On a side note here, sometimes it isn't "what to say" but "what to do," especially if you're at a bar. Not sure what to say? Buy them a drink! This goes for both men and women. It is an equal opportunity opener. In my, er, research, I have never witnessed someone turning down a free drink. See someone across the bar? Have the bartender send their next round over. Sitting next to someone you think is attractive that you want to talk to? Tell the bartender that you have their next tasty beverage. Even if they are drinking water, it is a great gesture to break the ice (over some ice!). See a smile? That's your sign that it is appreciated. At the very least, it has you on positive footing to start a conversation.

Still perplexed as to what you could use as an opening line? Let me give you a hand, or a line. Check out these suggestions based on the top flirting locations we discussed in chapter 2:

Opening Lines Based on Location

Group event or class (e.g., cooking, photography, art, cycling, etc.)	"You clearly have a talent for this. Maybe you can tutor me later."
Networking event	"Hi, I am_____, what brings you here tonight?
Seminar/Conference	"That was some really great information. We should compare notes!"
Airport	"So where are you running away to? Anywhere fun?"
Hotel bar	"Have you eaten here? I always like to get a recommendation when I travel."
Wedding	"Are you with the bride or groom? Or are you just crashing the wedding?"
Gym	"Do you know how to change the settings on this?"
Dog park	"Your dog is adorable! What is his name?"
Church/Temple/Mosque	"That was a great sermon, don't you think?"
Coffee shop	"Time for my caffeine fix! What cup are you on?"

As you can see, these lines are pretty simple! It's all about using the environment around you to give you some sort of opening. The possibilities are endless in every situation. If you're at a loss for words, the next time you see someone you want to approach, take a moment and look around. Take note of how you are feeling. Is the weather uncharacteristically hot? Cold? Is the music great? Too loud? Are they drinking something that looks good? Are they wearing something unique like a cool leather jacket or a great piece of jewelry? These are all starting points for a great opening line. I could write a list of thousands of lines for you to pick from, but I have faith in you. I am convinced that you can find *something* to use to start that conversation. Even if it is just "Hi."

What not to say

I need to take a moment and discuss what NOT to say when approaching someone. I need you to promise to never ever purposely insult or "neg" anyone. In "pick-up artist" circles, there are some who purposely teach men to insult women, essentially with backhanded compliments like, "I love your blond hair, you just need to work on those roots," or "That is a great shirt, my mom has the same one," or "Nice nails, are they fake?" Nice, huh? There are hundreds of these online, available for your reading displeasure. Or if you'd like to view it in action, check out *Crazy, Stupid, Love*. Ryan Gosling actually studied these techniques for the movie, but he kept my love for him alive by talking about how ridiculous the method is in several media interviews. <3 you RyRy.

Apparently there are men who believe that women (especially attractive women) need to be put down a notch in order for them to have a shot at dating them (or at least sleeping with them, which is the primary focus of many of these lessons). The theory is that these attractive women have their guard up because they are constantly hit on, and this is a surefire way to break through the clutter.

I hate this theory. I hate that it is taught. I hate that people actually listen to and implement it. I hate that it actually works on people, people who are already dealing with low self-esteem (which then plummets further). That's a lot of hate from someone who doesn't hate much of anything. Negs and insults have no business in flirting or dating. They are cruel and hurtful and just rude. So do me a favor and keep it classy.

Flirting Tip #19

Starting a conversation is as easy as "Hi"—just play nice—or I will find you.

Some Last Words about First Words

It almost doesn't matter what you say to your new acquaintance. It is how you approach the person, the confidence you show, and how you say whatever it is you're saying. Don't be afraid to say anything that comes to mind, as long as it's positive and makes the connection. Don't let another opportunity pass you by!

GET FEARLESS

- Find an icebreaker that works for you and own it, even if it's just "Hi" with a smile.
- Use anything in your environment as the source of an opening line as long as it's positive and light.
- Never insult someone as a way of flirting.

7
Speaking the Language

"I speak two languages, Body and English."
- Mae West

Body language is an extremely important piece in the flirting puzzle. Learning about it can teach you how you can use it to show others that you are interested in them, but also to see if they are interested in you. There are many cues that people give when flirting to show they like you, from subconscious indications via their body language to explicit verbal cues. A good flirt will bring all of those signals together to determine whether there is a potential connection.

Reading another person's body language can inform you how they feel about you without their saying a word. Of your body's two languages, your verbal language is conscious and deliberate, whereas your nonverbal or body language is out of your control. The "language" your body speaks is most often an automatic reaction to your emotions and without effort on your part. Your body language actually says more to someone subconsciously than your verbal words. You could say absolutely nothing and still make an impression. Being able to read someone's nonverbal clues is like being able to speak another language, and can give you a leg up in any romantic situation.

You may already have certain subconscious reactions to the way people speak to you with their bodies, but this chapter will allow you to *consciously* understand what they are saying. This can make or break your flirting game. Just to be clear with you—this is not meant to be an exhaustive explanation about body language or the interpretation of it—this is a quick fix. There are hundreds of books and programs dedicated to the subject, and if you're interested in really understanding and becoming an expert in body language, I suggest you continue your education, because it is fascinating stuff.

Flirting Tip #20

Take a moment to study the object of your affection's body language. It will tell you what they're not saying out loud!

So let's talk about how to read body language to understand whether someone is interested in you or not. Being able to read another's nonverbal cues can save you a lot of time, and even prevent rejection. This interpretation can help you to determine whether or not a touch is appropriate, if further conversations are worthwhile, or whether you should ask for a phone number or a date. There are certain things that men and women do differently in terms of body language, and we will parse some of those differences. However, for the most part, the cues are quite similar.

Below are the top body language cues to look for when you are in a flirting situation.

Gender-Neutral Body Language Signals of Interest:

- **Squared off shoulders**—If they are positioned so that it seems as if you are opening your hearts to each other, it is a sign that you are receptive and interested in hearing what they have to say. It says loud and clear that "I am listening, and I want to connect with you"—without your having to utter a syllable.

- **Leaning forward**—If she is leaning towards you it shows that she is interested and excited about what you have to say. Leaning back shows disinterest or dominance.

- **Open and animated gestures**—Is he expressive and using hand gestures to make points and tell stories? This shows that he is excited to talk to you.

- **Lip licking**—Unless they have some leftover barbecue sauce on their lips, lip-licking can reveal a physical attraction.

- **Flared nostrils**—If you are flirting with someone and those nostrils are flaring—watch out! It means that you are looking quite delectable.

- **Open arms**—Crossing your arms in front of your chest immediately sends a message that you are not interested, or you're opposed to what they are saying.

- **Mirroring**—Instead of doing it, you are now on the lookout for it. If the object of your affection is in sync with your movements, they are interested. Mirroring gives them a sense of comfort and connection because it feels familiar to them. People like people like them. So, how do you mirror? It's actually pretty easy—your companion is doing all the work, and you're just copying them. Follow their body movements, and a few seconds later, do the same thing. If they cross their legs, you cross your legs; if they lean back, you lean back; if they pick up their drink, you pick up your drink, all a couple seconds behind. It's like playing monkey see, monkey do—for grownups.

- **Pointy feet**—This is my favorite! Even when people try to hide their feelings and adjust their body language, their feet rarely lie. If his or her feet are pointed at you, this means that they are interested.

- **Raised eyebrows**—Raised eyebrows when you approach can be a sign of interest. It can also mean "Are you serious?" so try to look for another signal as well.

- **Eye contact/Smiling**—You are probably sick of hearing this phrase by now, but eye contact and smiling are the keys to the city. You are golden, so get on over there!

- **Dilated pupils**—Speaking of eyes, if their pupils dilate, research has shown that can be a sign they find you attractive.

- **Preening**—Are they fixing their hair or adjusting their clothing? Playing with her earrings or fixing his tie? Preening is all about trying to make yourself look better, because you like someone.

- **Laughter**—If they laugh at your jokes, no matter how silly or unfunny, you've got an interested party in your presence.

- **Light touches**—This is a fairly obvious sign of flirting. Lightly touching someone's arm, knee or shoulder shows interest. It's a nonverbal signal that they are open and friendly.

- **Head tilt**—The head tilt is a classic come-hither move that shows interest.

As you see, there are many subconscious cues that we give to people we're interested in. There are also several visual cues that we give off differently, based on our genders. When it comes to body language, men and women can be as different as strawberry and mint chocolate chip. I actually find gender variances in this area extremely interesting, because it turns out that these differences are really hard-wired. They've been in existence since the time when the earliest humans—cavemen and cavewomen—were getting their flirt on, although the differences then weren't exactly the same differences we see now. For example, then, things were a bit less complicated—the alpha male found the fertile female and threw her over his shoulder to carry her off for a little procreation action. Thankfully we have evolved … somewhat. Let's break it down so that you know exactly what he or she is silently saying.

Signs that Chicks Give

- **Hair twirling**—Hair twirling can be a subconscious sign of nervousness (maybe she thinks you are *that* cute), but it can also be a come-hither signal. Funny enough, many men find hair twirling to be profoundly annoying, but some of us just can't help it. So guys, even if it bugs you, it is still sending a signal, and it would be to your disadvantage to ignore it.

- **Crossed legs**—If she crosses her leg and her top leg points in your direction, she is interested. If the top leg points away, she might not be (or maybe she just had to switch legs to prevent a cramp…you'll have to investigate a little further to find out).

- **Wandering fingers**—If a woman has a drink and she's attracted to you or even getting a little hot and bothered, she may start to rub the bottom of the glass with her fingertips, or stroke the stem of the wine glass. If she doesn't have a drink, buy her one and see what happens!

- **Touchy Feely**—Especially from a woman, a touch can mean a lot. In a flirting situation, it is one of the most accurate signals that she's interested.

- **Shoe dance**—Dangling her shoe off from her toes is a way of showing that she's comfortable in the situation, and possibly there is an indication of a willingness to take off more than just her heels.

Signs that Guys Give

- **Guidance**—As you are walking together he "guides" you by touching the small of your back or your elbow. It's a mixture of "Back off, I've got her" to other guys, "I am not going to lose sight of this one" to himself, and "I am going to protect you" to the girl.

- **Hands on hips**—He is trying to accentuate his physical size and confidence (or build up his confidence if he is lacking). Oh, and he also is trying to direct your attention somewhere in the nether regions.

- **Puffed up**—If he is standing with his muscles contracted and at full attention he is trying to imprvess you with his stature.

- **Legs spread**—Whether you want it or not, he is sitting across from you giving you a crotch display to indicate what he has got to offer.

- **Tie stroking/hair smoothing/sock adjusting**—Guys preen too—they are trying to look good for you because they are interested.

- **Eyebrow flash**—If a guy is interested he will lift his eyebrows and crinkle his forehead. Just for a quick instant, though.

- **Spread those legs**—If a guy is into you, he will make a stand. Literally. If he squares off to you while standing with

his legs shoulder-width apart, he is looking to mate. Maybe just for tonight, though, so hose him down if necessary.

All of the above "cues" are generalizations based on what a "typical" reaction would be, given the extensive research available. I would warn against making any rash decisions based solely on whether or not you see one or two of these indicators, though. Patrick made that mistake for years, until he was called out on it....

Patrick thought he had it all figured out. He had read a couple of books on body language and thought he knew how to read women like those books. However, Patrick only focused in on learning what body language to look for, and what it meant. He skipped the part of the book that told him how to put it all together to make a real assessment of the situation. Armed with his so-called "information," Patrick went out, often. He would pay fervent attention to everything the women did while he was talking to them, and if he saw a glimpse of a shoe dance or a raised eyebrow, he went in for more. Sometimes "more" was a kiss, sometimes it was a touch, and sometimes "more" was him asking for a phone number. He was often rejected.

Patrick's problem was that he failed to take into account the other signals these women were giving him. When looking in retrospect, he talked about how some women seemed to be barely paying attention to him and facing away—but they were playing with their necklace, so he thought they must like him! Others were talking to their friends more than him, but they were twirling their hair, so he figured it was a done deal. Oh, so wrong, Patrick!

Assessing the situation as a whole is always the best move, especially combined with some common sense. A general rule for reading body language is to read in clusters—look for 2 or 3 different cues to put together an assessment. Also take a look at what they are doing and combine it with what they are saying. Use the body language as indicators but not as the only decisive factor. Oh, and don't spend so much time analyzing his or her every move so that you stop having fun! The worst thing you can do is to pay so much attention to their movements and micro-movements that they actually notice you noticing them. Use your interpretation of their body language as the wonderful tool that it is, nothing more.

GET FEARLESS

- Use body language to get an idea if they are interested in you.
- Don't make any rash decisions based on one or two signals, but use the indicators to figure out if there is a possible connection.

Flirting Tip #21

Look for clusters of signs when analyzing body language—don't focus on just one.

8

That's Why They Make Strawberry and Mint Chocolate Chip

"You got to know when to hold 'em, know when to fold 'em, Know when to walk away and know when to run."
- Kenny Rogers

In spite of your undeniable charisma and all around amazingness, there will be people who just won't appreciate your flirtations, and you need to know when to walk away. This chapter isn't going to be the most fun, but the information in it is essential. Regardless of how amazing you and I know you are, there are people out there who just don't recognize your worth. It is their loss, and you need to politely thank them for the conversation and move on to somebody who has a better chance of appreciating you and everything you have to offer.

The goal of this chapter is the opposite of the previous, because it focuses on reading people to understand when they are not interested. This is kind of the other "bookend." Wouldn't it save you a ton of heartache if you knew almost immediately if someone was not going to be interested? Reading these cues is a fear-buster! The fear of being rejected can almost be completely eliminated, because you will be able to make a judicious timely exit.

Guys are typically much worse at reading the signs that a woman isn't into them. They tend to miss a lot of the cues that should let them know it's time move on. This was actually substantiated in a study done jointly by Yale and Indiana University. The researchers tested 280 heterosexual male and female students by having each test subject sort photos of women into four categories—*sexually interested, friendly, sad, or rejected.* The men misidentified 12 percent of the images as *sexually interested.* Both sexes had difficulties distinguishing the difference between *friendly* and *sexually interested,* but men *again* were the worse of the two. Do guys just assume that anyone who is being nice to them really wants to sleep with them? Maybe...

A word to the wise about fear here—fear can literally put blinders on anyone who's trying to read the clues that people are giving you, even when they say loud and clear that they are not interested. The fear of rejection is strong, and often people (especially men) will ignore the signs that there just isn't a spark, because they don't want to be rejected. You would think the opposite would be more true—that fear would prevent people from approaching and connecting altogether, but that is not always the case. It is important to understand that learning about and opening your eyes to these cues can almost prevent the possibility of rejection completely! Take my client Ray, for example...

Ray is a great guy, recently divorced, good looking and with a lot to offer. However, Ray suffered from "delusional male syndrome." See, the problem was that Ray was so afraid of being hurt that he put on the blinders before he plunged forward into the dating pool. He had to be hit over the head with the proverbial bat to understand that a woman wasn't interested in him.

God bless his efforts, the man would talk to anyone and everyone—he just didn't know when to walk away, despite obvious body language that showed him no interest whatsoever. After finally learning to open his eyes, Ray is focusing his efforts on women who are interested, and making a hasty retreat from those who are not. He is less fearful, more self-aware, and the bonus is he feels better than ever about himself because he has been connecting with women who actually like him, instead of wasting his time where he's unappreciated.

There are plenty of fish in the sea, but if they are swimming away from you, it is probably a sign that they are not the fish for you.

THEY JUST AREN'T INTO YOU

So what are the cues that people give when they're just not interested? As I said, this is really worth understanding, because they can save you a lot of time by keeping you from staying in a conversation a moment longer than you should. So, if you see some of these scenarios pop up? Move on to someone who deserves you. Here are the top ten things to look for when you are having a conversation that just should be put out of its misery:

1. **They just aren't listening.** At all. If you are trying to hold a conversation with someone and they're zoning out, watching the TV in the back of the bar, making faces at their friend, or staring blindly in any direction other than yours, this conversation is going nowhere. When someone is interested in you, they are engaged with you. They are listening to what you have to say, and asking questions in return. So if you are having a one-sided conversation about that restaurant that you would really love to go back to, this isn't the guy or gal you'll be going there with. Frankly, be thankful that they aren't interested—if they are completely ignoring you during conversation (without a medical excuse), they are just rude.

2. **Their body is completely turned away from you.** A cold shoulder is a pretty clear bad sign. If you're having a conversation with someone and they are not facing you

directly, or worse, they are almost entirely turned around, there is nothing that is going to save this. Time to walk away and find someone who is willing to give you their full frontal.

3. **They never touch you.** If the touch barrier is still in place, there is something missing here. It doesn't have to be much, but some type of contact is necessary.

4. **They aren't talking with you, but at you.** Are you with someone who is blabbing away about themselves, and not asking you a single question? Then they probably are not interested in you. People who like you want to get to know you. They will ask you questions and let you speak.

Just a quick side note on this: there are also people out there who are so self-absorbed, that even though they like you, they will still spend 99% of the time talking about themselves. We call them narcissists. Narcissists tend to focus all interpersonal exchanges on themselves, lack empathy, and love for people to love them. They might try to date you, love you, marry you, but in the end you will always be in second place—to them. It depends if you're willing to put up with that. If you are, it's your decision to continue that conversation. However, that selfishness likely translates far beyond communications, so tread carefully.

1. **They start a conversation with other people rather than just keeping it to the two of you.** When they start a side conversation with your friend, or work really hard to bring their friends into your bubble, the connection is doomed. When someone is interested, they are focused. They are looking to connect with you and only

you. Once someone starts bringing others into the conversation, it's a telltale sign that they are looking for an out. Move on, and find someone willing to stay with you one-on-one.

2. **They flirt with others.** What is worse than when they invite others into your conversation? When they flirt with those other people. Unless they are the type of person that flirts with anything that has a pulse (um, me), flirting with another person in front of you is a death sentence for your connection. If you happen to be flirting with a super flirt, you need to use your amazing sleuth skills (learned in this book!) to decipher if the object of your affection is romantically flirting with others, or if they are just trying to be charming and irresistible…to the world.

3. **They put you in the "friend zone."** Okay, so they might not come right out and say "I am not interested," but they will use their words to let you know that this just isn't happening. If the "friend" word is thrown around a lot, that is a bad sign. For example, you might hear, "I am always looking to meet new friends," or "A bunch of us head out there once a month just as friends, you should join us." The friend zone is hard to get out of.

4. **They liken you to a sibling.** Worse than "friend zone" is when they bring you right into the family fold. If he or she says *you are just like my sister (or brother)*, it is never ever going to happen.

5. **They don't close.** By close I mean ask for a number, ask for a date, ask for ANYTHING that will continue the conversation. Now you may be saying, "What if they are

---

Flirting Tip #22

There are cues to show you when it just isn't working. Learn to recognize and accept them so you can move on and find someone new.

---

too shy?" or "What if they don't know how?" Whether you are the guy, or whether you're the woman talking to the guy, if the guy doesn't close, there is no interest. He is simply not interested in having anything beyond this conversation. Don't get me wrong, girls can close too, but typically, the woman is going to expect the guy to seal the deal. So enjoy it for the practice that it has been, and then find yourself someone who is going to pursue you beyond that initial flirtation.

6. **They go to the bathroom … and never return.** You probably are wondering why this is even on the list. Well, it's here because of a story Ryan told me. He was talking with Simone, a girl that he was completely uninterested in. In an effort to avoid hurting her feelings, he excused himself to go to the bathroom. Instead of going back to Simone, when he came out of the bathroom he went back to hang out with his buddies. Simone, however, found Ryan with his friends on the other side of the bar and

tried to pick right back up with their conversation. Bad move. If someone you are talking to goes to the bathroom and doesn't return, *please please please* do not seek them out. They are not interested and they are just plain rude—and you are so much better than that!

Handling Rejection

Try not to take any of these situations personally. These are all initial flirtations, and not relationships. The best part is, they are all great practice! You can use what you learn on the next person, and become even more confident in your delivery and ability to read people. The purpose is to flirt with as many people that you are attracted to as possible, and then see who in turn is attracted to you as well. My friend Alex has the best attitude when it comes to rejection. If the woman he's talking to tells or shows him that she's not interested, he considers it a favor. Clearly if she isn't into him, she has no sense or no taste or maybe none of either one. No need to waste any time on anyone like that!

I like to think of flirting as shopping. You are going to try on a lot of shirts and some of them won't fit. Some of them will make you look fat, some will be itchy or uncomfortable, but there will be a few that are a perfect fit. So just think of these other "shirts" that don't fit as rejected clothing. You make the decision. Put them to the side where they deserve to be, and move on back to the rack for more browsing. Eventually you will find your perfect fit, and when you do, you can appreciate it even more.

Rejection sucks, but learn from every experience so your next flirtation is even better. Plenty of fish out there!

Flirting Tip #23

Rejection sucks, but learn from every experience so your next flirtation is even better. Plenty of fish out there!

Rejection is going to happen, but there is a right and wrong way to go about accepting it. I like to classify these ways as *trashy* and *classy*. Trashy involves insulting, drink throwing, or any other way of visibly getting upset. Classy is when you take it in stride and move on towards greener pastures. Here are my tips for keeping it classy:

- **Be gracious**—Be gracious and kind, even if they are not. Thank them for talking to you. It will not only leave a lasting impression on them, but you can sleep better for knowing you are a decent person.

- **Pretend it didn't even faze you**—Don't get all pissed off and show it. Walk away with a smile on your face, and move on knowing that it was their loss.

- **Remain confident**—Don't let one bad experience bring you down. Keep the faith—dating is a numbers game, and eventually you will find the right combination.

- **Take notes**—Learn something if you can. Think about things you can do differently the next time. Maybe you came on too strong, maybe you tried to be funny (but you aren't), maybe you went way out of your league...life is all about learning from your mistakes. There is a lesson in every situation.

Before we get off the subject, I would also like to take a second to talk about rejection online. Online dating can be very disheartening when you are spending time and energy contacting people, but receiving no response or perhaps a negative reply in return. Dealing with rejection online is all about reframing how you think about it. These men or women out there in cyberspace simply do not know you. They barely know anything about you. Any online rejection should be taken with a grain of salt, and your efforts should be redirected to those who do respond and engage with you. No response? No worries. There are millions of others who can take their place.

If I drive nothing else home, please heed this:

Don't let the fear of rejection get in the way of you getting your flirt on.

There are plenty of fish in the sea and there is someone for everyone. It's a numbers game, baby!

What About When You Aren't Interested?

Of course, there are going to be times when you're the one who isn't interested. You have used your super flirt skills, and they are working, but you realize that they are being used on the wrong person. Maybe they aren't your type, or their breath stinks, their voice is annoying, or you just could never imagine yourself kissing them. It is going to happen (of course it is going to happen! how could everyone in the world be your type?), but how you react and handle the situation will make all the difference.

When you suddenly realize that you have no interest in the person you are flirting with, you need to immediately take a step back in terms of your use of the five super flirt skills. Just as you would not want to be led on by someone not interested in you, you don't want to lead anyone else on. It doesn't mean that you have to go stone cold, but just tailor back your smiling, eye contact, body language signals, flirty conversation, and touch. Typically, this pullback will be all that is necessary for the conversation to end organically.

What happens if you have done all of that and they are still chatting away? I am not a proponent of lying to get out of the situ-

Flirting Tip #24

Not interested? Keep it classy and bow out respectfully.

ation, but I am huge fan of excusing yourself from the conversation. There is an extremely simple way to do this that doesn't offend people. Instead of excusing yourself to go to the bathroom and never coming back (which we learned is not always 100% effective as demonstrated above, and it's not very nice, besides), simply say, "It's been nice talking to you, I hope you have an amazing night, but I need to get back to my friends." In doing that you are respectfully ending the conversation without saying to them, "I don't like you because you are ugly, fat, not my type, talk too much, have a squeaky voice, or seem dumb." There's never a need to literally tell someone that they are not enough for you. I believe in flirting karma. So put out into the universe what you want to get back. If you are a good person and treat others well, you will be treated well in return. Keep it classy and carry on!

GET FEARLESS

- Know the signs that someone is not interested so you can make a hasty retreat—with your chin up.

- Be respectful to people—whether they aren't interested in you, or you are not interested in them. Keep it classy.

9

What the Heck Do I
Do Now?

*"The amount of good luck coming your way depends on
your willingness to act."*
- Barbara Sher

So what happens after you've been flirting for a while and feel a spark? What goes on after you connect with someone, neither of you has run away, and the night, event, or conversation is naturally coming to a close? Well, someone needs to close the deal.

In order to close the deal, one of you (and typically this falls on the man) asks for a phone number and/or asks to set up a date. This is when the real fear tends to set in. It's all fun and games until you meet somebody that you actually like, who has the same interests as you, and who you can see spending more time with. Suddenly you're invested (to an extent), and if they do not accept your further advances, it's going to hurt. But if you don't try, you lose out completely. Push your fear to the side and make a move. Now, let's talk about deal closers that work.

GETTING THE DIGITS

Guys, if you are looking to close the deal, it's really pretty easy. You've already determined whether or not she is interested in you. You have read her body language, listened to what she's been saying, and you have a good gut feeling. If the two of you have been talking for any significant amount of time (over an hour), she is going to *expect* you to ask for her number. So simply go for it. My favorite way to have a guy close the deal is to do a combo—ask for the number, but only to confirm a date. For example, if you are talking to a woman, getting a great vibe, and want to see her again, set the date right then! Say something like, "What are you doing next Saturday night? Let's grab dinner," and she then gives you her number so you can get all the details figured out during the days in between. A little take-charge attitude goes a long way and can be super sexy.

Flirting Tip #25

Close the deal. At some point, you need to ask for their phone number or give them yours.

If those scenarios are too forward, you can always just ask for her number and continue the conversation before committing to a "real" date. A simple, "I'd love to take you out sometime, why don't you give me your number and I'll give you a call" can work magically. It has the promise of a date, and you are taking control of the situation (which is what she expects), and closing the deal (which is what I expect from you). Under no circumstances should you simply say, "Can I have your number?" or "Why don't you give me your number?" Give her a purpose for handing over her digits—inspire her a bit.

Now, ladies, this isn't to say that you cannot be an active participant in the closing. Firstly, you can provide him with all of the verbal hints that let him know you want to see him again. This includes comments such:

- "I'd love to see you again."
- "I don't want this conversation to end."
- "There's this great bar we should check out next time."
- "I'm dying to try out this new restaurant—do you like Thai?"
- "We would make beautiful babies together."

Okay, you can see through me. Just kidding on that last one.

If your verbal clues don't work, and he still isn't going for it, you can hand him your number yourself. I am all for women going after what they want, but I am also a proponent of guys being the aggressor when it comes to moving the relationship along if you have been connecting and having a conversation. However, there are times when the guy IS interested and still isn't closing the deal. I have talked with and coached so many men who either felt they were out of their league or didn't think she was into them (when she was) and didn't ask for the number. There are simply times where you have to take into your own hands, ladies. Ask the bartender for a pen or dig one out of your purse, give him your number, and tell him that you would love for him to call you sometime. It is forward, but not aggressive. You have been connecting, after all, and you weren't going to let his courage (or temporary lack thereof) get in the way of seeing where this could go.

It really does work either way, but I am speaking from my experience of talking to thousands of women, that women prefer the men to close. However, talking to thousands of men, they prefer not to hit their head against the wall. So if the ladies can make it a little easier on them, they are all for it. No matter what, someone has to do the work and close, or a possibly amazing connection could be wasted.

A note on when to set the date: if you didn't do the number/date combo, I suggest setting up a date within seven days of that initial flirtation. Going back into gender roles, the guy should call the woman within 1 to 3 days of meeting to plan the date and time. The date shouldn't be the day after the call, but it also shouldn't be two weeks later. You need enough time for suspense to build, but not too much time that the feelings you have start to fizzle out.

GET FEARLESS

- Seal the deal—get the digits, give the digits, and make a date.
- Guys, don't be afraid to do a date/digit combo—ask for her number to confirm an already planned date.
- Ladies, don't be hesitant to hand him your number if you have the right vibe. It's the 21st century!

THE FIRST DATE

Once you have the date set up, the real fun starts! First dates are my favorite, especially after that initial flirtation, and you know what you can look forward to. Heck, I think all first dates are fun! The two of you being together is exciting and new, full of possibilities, and without any real pressure other than to have fun.

There are certain things that you can do to ensure an amazing first date, and a few things to avoid. Let's get to the list:

1. **Pick a fun and casual restaurant.** Wherever you go should be a casual restaurant. I'm not talking something as casual as fast food McDonald's here, but somewhere that you can go, relax and have a conversation. It shouldn't be too stuffy, too fancy, or too loud. Some people love to plan those fun adventurous first dates that involve rock climbing, surfing, cycling, or amusement parks, but I would rather you hit up a local Ruby Tuesday before one of those options. Fun and adventurous dates

are great, but right now you need an opportunity to get to know each other through conversation (which you cannot have while sky diving).

2. **Gussy up, casually.** I just love that word. Not sure why. Anywho, you should look your absolute best, but don't go overboard. Dress appropriately for the location of the date, but wear what makes you feel the most confident.

3. **Keep it light.** Continue to keep the conversation light. You can get a tiny bit deeper than you did during your first conversation, but it still should be kept light and positive. This is not the time to start delving into any psychological issues that you or anyone in your family may have—it is about putting your best foot forward and talking about all your wonderful qualities, hopes and dreams.

4. **Flirt!** Don't forget to continue to implement all of the flirting tips from chapter 5. Just because you got the date, it doesn't mean that flirting stops. In fact it never stops. Ever. I want you to be flirting when you are 80 years old and married. So when you are on the date, remember the 5 steps to super flirt:

   - Smile

   - Make lots of eye contact

   - Have good conversation

   - Use your body language

   - Touch

5. **Turn your phone off—All the way off!** There is no greater turn-off on a date than someone who checks their phone every 5 minutes in front of you. Emergencies only here. Real emergencies. Like people bleeding.

6. **Do not get drunk.** It might be tempting to let loose and have a few more than normal, but this is not the time or the place to do that. Stick to the two-drink rule so you can remember the conversation in the morning and avoid any regrets.

7. **He pays.** Sorry, guys, but the first three or four dates are completely on you. It is going to be expected and if it doesn't happen she's probably going to think that you're rude or cheap. I will admit that this is an archaic way of thinking. Many women are making just as much or sometimes more money than men, however, it is still expected that the guy will be the one to pull out the wallet at first. Ladies, you shouldn't just sit there and accept it. You should at least *pretend* to offer to pay for the first date. A couple of dates down the road you should absolutely be splitting, especially if you're in similar financial circumstances, but for now it is all him. Research has shown that women expect to be treated for the first couple dates, and when the guy doesn't pay or asks the woman to split, he is often seen as cheap. I am not saying that this is right, but it is what is commonly "expected." I am a believer that the guy pays for the first date to keep chivalry alive, but that there is a give and take after that point (unless one partner makes little to

nothing and the other a ton—then Moneybags should cover most dating expenses).

8. **Do not have sex.** I repeat: do not have sex. I do not care how turned on those kisses get you; do not have sex. There may be stories about how one-night stands can lead to relationships, but for the most part they burn out fast and the people move on. Do you want to grow a long-lasting relationship? Then a good night kiss is fine, but leave it outside the door. I am not a coach who is going to tell you that you should be in a committed relationship before you have sex, but it definitely shouldn't be on the first date. Oxytocin is a powerful hormone that releases in women during sex and can start to complicate everything due to its effects on women's emotions. It has been called the "love hormone" and can make a woman feel a little more bonded and attached than she would be without having the big O. So it is best to put that off for a second to keep your head clear. Speaking of keeping your head clear, remember that alcohol lowers your inhibitions considerably and may lead to decisions that wouldn't always be the same sober. Make sure you remain in complete control of the situation, and: Do. Not. Have. Sex.

GET FEARLESS

- Make your first date one to remember—pick a fun location where it's possible that you can have an actual conversation.
- Don't forget to flirt.
- And don't have sex!

THE KISS

So you had a great first date, you are getting all the signs that he or she is into you. What about the ever important first kiss? That kiss can make or break your chance at moving an inch further in your new romance. I have met many people (both men and women) who have ended a budding relationship because the kissing wasn't cutting it. Your kiss is the gateway to sexual chemistry. A good kiss has been shown to raise your levels of serotonin, which is a serious mood booster, and dopamine, which is a pleasure overloader and can actually make you crave more kisses. This is serious business! Many women evaluate whether or not they would have sex with a guy based on the kiss. If that kiss is terrible, it will be extremely difficult for her to move past it. Men can be slightly less particular (depending on the opportunity that presents itself), but in my experience the kiss has always been important to everyone.

So the million-dollar question becomes, "What makes a great kiss?" Well here are five tips to take into account before you pucker up:

1. **Start slow and cycle**—Don't rush right into things and get your tongue involved. Start soft and slow, just lips, and warm up to using your tongue. Cycle back to just lips, and enjoy the dance.

2. **Control the waterworks**—The number one complaint I hear (and sadly have experienced) is the sloppy wet kiss. Your kiss shouldn't be dry, but you aren't looking to rehydrate your partner either. If you are leaving her face

shiny after a make out session, you need to try and hold back some of that saliva.

3. **Touch**—A good kiss involves touch. Touch your partner's face, pull them into you, or hold their arms—anything to connect you physically beyond your lips and show your passion.

4. **Be passionate but not aggressive**—If you have been kissing for a few minutes, spice it up with moments of passion with harder/faster kisses, but return to the soft sensual way you started. Avoid clashing teeth at all costs.

5. **Pay attention to your breath**—All the chemistry in the world cannot mask garlic breath. Don't ruin that first kiss with something that could be resolved with a Tic Tac.

Either one of you can initiate the kiss. Just pay attention to their actions that lead up to that point, because it can feel pretty awkward if you go for the lips and get a cheek. Are they talking closer? Leaning in? Touching you? Use all of the indicators we have talked about to gauge whether it's the right time. Got a green light? Lean in slowly and wait for them to reciprocate to start the lip lock.

Just a note: don't ever stop kissing. Research has shown that kissing can be used as a barometer of whether your relationship is happy and healthy. So keep making out and enjoy the effects of those neurotransmitters.

GET FEARLESS

- Having a great date and want to take it to the next level? Go in for the kiss—but be prepared, it is important!

- Keep on kissing—make sure to keep making out to keep your relationship hot.

THE DATING MINDSET

From the first date on, the best advice I can give is to keep the right dating mindset. It can make or break a relationship (I am using the word "relationship" very loosely to describe someone new that you're dating) and is the reason why many of my coaching clients have had problems in the past. Many issues can arise during a relationship due to a wrong frame of mind, but there are some that come up the most frequently in my practice. In my experience these love-lost individuals either 1) played it too cool or 2) wanted to go from 0 to 60 in two dates. They were then left wondering why the person they were dating disappeared. Take Kevin, for example....

Kevin is a great catch. He is 34, smart, funny, and super attractive. He has never had a problem meeting women, getting numbers, or going on dates. His problem was maintaining those relationships. Kevin is a romantic at heart and was desperate to have a relationship like his parents— who had enjoyed 40 years of wedded bliss after a very short courtship. The problem was that he put that expectation on every date he had. It would be the first date and he would make "jokes" during the date about running off to get married before the night ended. By the second date he was talking kids, and often before the first month was up he was asking them to move in.

Sure, he had chemistry with these women, but chemistry can only go so far. Eventually each relationship dissolved because either he realized that there was no long-term potential, or she got freaked out by how fast things were moving. Nothing lasted beyond 3 months, and he found himself perpetually single. Until he changed his attitude. Just recognizing his habits and the reasons for them helped him to change his mindset and slow things down. He eventually found a woman that he took his time to get to know, and ended up moving in with...after a year.

Do you see any of Kevin in you? Or maybe the opposite? Like my friend Kim...

Kim is a gorgeous divorced 42-year-old, who has more men interested in her than days in the year. However, Kim's marriage took a toll on her feelings about love. She no longer feels that she is worthy of love or that she is going to find a loving relationship. Due to those feelings, she will not open up emotionally to the guy she is dating for months. By that time, the guy usually has broken up with her because his feelings aren't being reciprocated.

Neither works. Each of those scenarios is based on the mindset in which Kevin and Kim entered their new relationship. "Kevins" put their pedal to the metal and jump in full throttle wearing rose-colored glasses, and "Kims" use their fear of being hurt to keep everyone at arm's length.

Understanding your current mindset can help you turn it around to replace it with one that works. There are some basic

Flirting Tip #26

Your mindset will change everything. Get the right atti-tude and you might end up in the right relationship.

things to keep in mind to ensure that your attitude is where it needs to be to stay happy and healthy while dating:

Keep it in perspective. Keep it cool when you start to date someone. Enjoy their company, get to know them, but don't place any pressure on the situation. Granted, there are people who meet, fall in love, and marry within a few weeks. The majority of relationships, however, take time to grow. Don't place anyone else's timeline on your relationship. Recognize that the first 4 to 6 months of any relationship is the honeymoon phase where everyone is on their best behavior. It takes time to get to know someone and to open up, and it takes time to fall in love. Take the time.

Keep meeting and dating. You have just met, and you it's too early to be closing yourself off to other opportunities. Continue to date. Continue to meet people. Continue to flirt. It typically takes 6 to 8 dates before a couple decides to have an exclusive relationship. Until you're in an exclusive relationship, the best thing is to keep things at a modest pace and to date others. It keeps you from getting in too deep too fast, or becoming clingy. From either a woman's or a man's perspective, there is nothing less attractive and clingy and overbearing.

Keep yourself. Don't lose yourself in the relationship. A healthy relationship includes two wholes, so it is important that you maintain your own identity and don't immediately (don't ever!) turn entirely into an "us" and disregard your "I." Stay in touch with your friends, and make time for them. Have a girl's night or a boy's weekend; make a regular lunch date with your best friend. Just don't isolate yourself. Understand that you are an amazing individual regardless of who is on your arm. Do not correlate your self-worth with whether or not you have a partner.

Keep yourself open. Open up to your date. On the first couple of dates it is better to keep things fairly superficial, but as you continue to see each other, let them see more of the real you. Talk about your dreams, your hopes, and your fears. Have real conversations that let them see who you really are. You are lovable. Don't forget it.

Keep an open mind. Do your best not to bring past relationships or past issues into your current relationship. We all do it to an extent, but try especially hard not to typecast your date based on a prior bad experience. If your ex was an alcoholic, don't assume your date is too because she had two drinks; if your ex was a liar, don't second-guess everything your date is saying; if your ex was ambivalent about you, don't assume that your date isn't dying to learn everything about you. Give them a couple of dates to start to show you who they are, and try not to judge based on the subtle suggestions that seem to be reminiscent of your past. This is absolutely the hardest but most essential thing to do when getting in the right frame of mind.

Keep flirting! Never stop flirting in your relationship. Flirting can keep your relationship exciting, and interesting, and hot. Remember, it is about making them feel good, and in return you get to feel good about yourself too. Pay compliments, leave sexy notes, use touch often, and practice lots of other ways to make your partner feel like the center of the universe.

GET FEARLESS

- Get in the right mindset to date—perspective is everything.

- Continue to date other people until you are exclusive.

- Keep an open mind, and keep prior relationships out of this one!

10

The Digital Flirt

"I don't believe in email. I'm an old-fashioned girl.
I prefer calling and hanging up."
- Sarah Jessica Parker

It would be wrong to write a book about flirting without addressing the fact that much of our flirtation may end up as a digital form of communication. It would almost be irresponsible to not talk about it. The majority of all Americans have mobile devices, and they are using them to text, Skype, e-mail, surf the internet, watch videos, etc. We are living in a digital age, and there are seemingly nonstop developments in ways to communicate and connect technologically. From the moment this book is written until it is released and again, to the time you're reading it (now!), it is guaranteed that new communication technologies will arise.

While some of those digital messages may be professional, the vast majority of our communications will be personal interactions. Texts to friends, emails to parents, Skype calls with your girlfriend—there is an enormous amount of personal communication being conducted over the airwaves. But watch out—this technology can becomes quite the double-edged sword. On one hand, it allows you to connect and flirt easier, quicker, and more often than ever before. On the flipside, you will now be leaving an un-retractable footprint, and regardless of whether you delete it from your phone, your computer, Facebook, tumblr, etc., there is a record of it somewhere, and because of that you need to understand how to protect yourself. It is all fun and games until someone gets caught with a picture of their wiener on Twitter.

Let's talk about the different ways that tech and flirtations interact in the four main avenues used while flirting and dating: text, email, Facebook and other social media, and Skype.

TEXT MESSAGING

Texting is likely to become your greatest flirtation tool ever. Flirtatious texting is so much fun because there is a distinctive lack of pressure. Remember when text and email didn't exist and you had to call someone up to talk to them? You would be so nervous, hoping that they would pick up, and left flustered if you had to leave a voice mail. The beauty of texting is there is no such pressure—no worries about catching someone at a bad time, or wondering if they were avoiding your call. You can simply send a fun text out into the universe and see what comes back. I personally love texting because it makes you feel like you're connecting, without feeling invasive or aggressive.

Flirting Tip #27

Using technology the right way can ignite a flirtatious spark, or keep the fires burning.

IMHO (and more on that later), all of your texts should either be either flirty or informative, only. Texting is not the place to discuss serious matters in love, business, or otherwise. It is, however, a place to confirm plans, make plans, or flirt. I have seen many relationships fail because of misinterpreted text messages. Your tone and inflection account for an enormous amount of how people interpret what you are saying—text takes that element away and is completely reliant on your words and the reader's interpretation. So if you keep it fun, flirty, or informative you should be safe.

Not sure how to flirt via text? Let's look at what a flirtatious round of messages could look like:

You: Hey, sexy—I had a great time last night!

Them: I had a blast. You are so funny. My sides still hurt.

You: Oh, I have many more qualities to show you next time—just wait ;)

Them: Counting the minutes :)

Or if you are a little further along in your relationship:

You: Hey you, what are you up to?

Them: Just about to climb into bed.

You: Mmmm that sounds fun—want company?

Them: How quickly can you get here? ;)

Or if you are reaaaally far along:

You: Thinking about you ... and your legs.

Them: You won't have to imagine for long, they will be wrapped around you later.

As you can see, flirtatious texts are all about the tease! They can range from G-rated to XXX, but the purpose is always to leave them wanting more.

Here are some of my parameters for texting the object of your affection. Keep in mind that some of them are only appropriate when you are actually in a relationship (see chapter 9):

- **Know when to stop.** Do not continue to text incessantly for hours—especially if you just met. Leave them hanging after 3 or 4 messages with a "Talk to you later" or "Gotta run—have a great day!" Texting may not be as invasive as a phone call, but it sure can be if it doesn't stop.

- **Keep it super short.** If your text breaks up into more than one message, it's too long.

- **Let them know that you are thinking about them.** A quick "Missing you!", "Can't wait to see you!" or "Thinking about you!" are great if you have had a couple dates and have built a rapport.

- **Keep it clean…at first.** When you just start talking to someone, all texts should remain PG. Sure you can tell them you can't stop thinking about them, can't wait to kiss them again, or love the way they smell, but no further than that. However, when you are in a committed exclusive relationship, the sky is the limit. Sexting can be a great way to spice it up—just, no pictures, please!

- **Never drunk-text.** Just because it is quick and easy doesn't mean you should be doing it after that fourth shot of tequila. Raise your hand if you have woken up the next morning and read texts you don't remember sending. Keep your hand up if those texts said things you would never say sober. Hide your phone from yourself if necessary.

- **Don't expect an immediate reply.** Just because he didn't write you back within five seconds doesn't mean he isn't interested. Not everyone is tethered to their phones, and a little time between texts is completely normal.

- **Remember the power of the forward.** Whatever you say can be used against you, and forwarded to everyone they know. So don't write anything that would completely horrify you if your mother (or your boss) read it.

- **Check your audience.** The biggest issue with an electronic communication can arise when it ends up in someone else's phone or inbox. My friend Tim once sent a dirty sext message meant for his girlfriend to his boss, by mistake. It wasn't pretty, and to this day it still embarrasses him. Don't let your haste to send a message prevent you from double-checking who you are sending it to.

- **Limit emoticons and abbreviations.** Unless you are under the age of 18, more than one emoticon in a text message is excessive. Likewise, abbreviations are acceptable (see the guide below), but should not be used to type entire sentences. Do you really think "GR8 2 CU 2DAY, CWTNT" is sexy? The English language is a beautiful thing—use it as often as you can.

Ah, abbreviations… Use of massive amounts of abbreviations used to be something that only teenagers did, but the disease has since spread to adults. Abbreviating words while texting is acceptable while flirting—*in very small quantities*—no more than one per text. Let your intelligence shine through by simply spelling most of your words out. The list of abbreviations frequently used is endless. I will admit that there have been times where I had to Google an abbreviation to figure out what the heck someone was trying to say to me. I'll try and save you a little time with the top 50 abbreviations that you may see while flirting:

1. 143—I love you (Wondering why? # of letters: 1 in I, 4 in LOVE, 3 in YOU)
2. 2DAY—today
3. 2moro—tomorrow
4. ADN—any day now

5. AFAIK—as far as I know

6. B4—before

7. B4N—bye for now

8. BRB—be right back

9. BTW—by the way

10. CWTNT—can't wait till next time

11. FWB—friends with benefits

12. FWIW—for what it's worth

13. FYEO—for your eyes only

14. GLHF—good luck, have fun

15. GR8—great

16. HTH—hope this helps / happy to help

17. IDK—I don't know

18. IKR—I know, right?

19. ILY—I love you

20. IMHO—in my humble opinion

21. IRL—in real life

22. IU2U—it's up to you

23. JK—just kidding

24. J4F—just for fun

25. JIC—just in case

26. JSYK—just so you know

27. K or KK—okay

28. L8R—later

29. LMAO—laughing my ass off

30. LOL—laughing out loud

31. NM—never mind

32. NMU—not much, you?

33. NP—no problem

34. NSFW—not safe for work
35. OMG—oh my god
36. ROTFLMAO—rolling on the floor laughing my ass off
37. SMH—shaking my head
38. SWAK—sealed with a kiss
39. SWYP—so, what's your problem?
40. THX or TX or THKS—thanks
41. TIA—thanks in advance
42. TIME—tears in my eyes
43. TLC—tender loving care
44. TMI—too much information
45. TMRW—tomorrow
46. TTYL—talk to you later
47. TY or TU—thank you
48. WTF—what the f***
49. WYWH—wish you were here
50. XOXO—hugs and kisses

*Note—these don't have to uppercase to translate—they can
   be lowercase or a mix

This list is far from exhaustive, so if you don't see something
you're looking for, Google away. You would be surprised what can
be conveyed with a few capital letters arranged together.

In sum, text messaging can be a great tool while flirting. Used
properly it can add a little fire and fun to your communications.
Used improperly, it can blow up a relationship, or worse. Tread
cautiously.

GET FEARLESS

- Use texts to stay in touch and keep the spark alive between dates.

- Keep texts short, clean and fun.
- Don't overuse abbreviations or emoticons in text messages.

E-MAIL

Email is also at the forefront of flirtations and can play a major role in any courtship or relationship. It is a great way to communicate and say a little bit more than a text message, but still not be as intrusive as a phone call. (As a side note here, please do not interpret my classification of phone calls as intrusive to mean you should not talk on the phone. On the contrary, I think regular phone calls are important. Voice is a very important component of any flirtation, and brings back the ever-important tone and inflection needed to communicate effectively. However, calling someone means that you take the risk of interrupting them during their day or missing them entirely, if you choose not to leave a message.) Texts and emails are simply easier to send as the recipient can multi-task while reading and replying.

As with text messages, you should avoid most serious topics, as the lack of inflection and the wide openness for interpretation can lead to some serious problems with construing the written word. And just because email provides room for unlimited characters doesn't mean you should fill them with your grievances. My client Jessica learned this the hard way...

Jessica had been dating Brad for six months, and things were going well. They both agreed that they were in an exclusive relationship, and that they loved each other. BUT there were certain things that Brad did that drove Jessica crazy. Things like: Brad would tell her that he would call at a specific time, but then he wouldn't call until an hour after that time; Brad would attend events for work where he could bring a date, but he didn't invite Jessica; and Brad never complimented Jessica on the way she looked when they went out. Clearly there were issues that needed to be addressed, but Jessica was scared to bring them up directly.

Instead, she decided to write a "Dear Brad" email. She went on to list everything Brad did that bothered her. She explained why she was upset, and how he could fix it. She pressed "Send." His reply? "Goodbye Jessica." Brad ended it there because he felt attacked without a forum to have a back-and-forth discussion. He walked away entirely that day and Jessica learned the hard way that email is not the forum for difficult issues of the heart.

Have you ever written a "Dear Brad" email? How did that go over? I would assume that most of the time, not so well. Human beings need a two-way forum to discuss touchy subjects. Talking to your boyfriend or girlfriend about things that bother you should never be blasted off in a one-way email. Take the time to do it in person, where your tone and inflection can soften the blow. The relationship might not work out anyway, but at least you are giving it a fighting shot.

What you can do in emails is have flirty and fun conversations that are a little more in-depth than a couple characters of text messaging. Emails to let someone know that you are thinking about them, to make plans to see each other again, or to thank them for a great time are perfectly acceptable. All other rules relating to text messaging also apply including:

- knowing when to stop the chain for the day
- checking your "To:" field carefully
- not expecting an immediate reply
- always remembering that your email can be shared with the click of a button

One additional rule about email is to *never ever* use your work email for flirting or personal use in general. Unless you want your boss to read all about what you plan on doing to your girlfriend when you get home that night, use your own devices (laptop, phone, tablet, etc.) to conduct any flirtatious activity. There has been precedent that allows your employer to record any and all activity/communications that you have on employer-owned equipment. Think that you are safe on Gmail or Hotmail? Not quite—it can all be recorded real-time and be permanently retained in your employer's log. I myself have witnessed people having personal communications used against them in an employment environment, all because the employee didn't know that their employer was monitoring their activities. Think twice before sext messaging if you have a company-issued phone.

Flirting Tip #28

Never use your work email or devices to flirt—Big Brother may be watching.

GET FEARLESS

- Keep your emails clean and fun.
- Never use your work email or company issued equipment for flirtatious correspondence.

SKYPE

Skype is one of the most brilliant technological advances ever. It allows you to connect face-to-face with someone and have a real conversation where you can see their facial expressions and hear their voice—all without having to leave your couch. The best part? It's free. If you are making Skype-to-Skype calls, you can talk all day long. All you need is a computer with an internet connection, and to download the program.

Skype is especially helpful in long-distance relationships or if you have a job where you travel a lot. Did you meet someone on that singles cruise? You can stay in touch via Skype. Connect with someone in a nearby city that you cannot see during the week? Set up a Skype date every Wednesday. Travel once a month? Skype from your hotel to say goodnight.

FaceTime on the iPhone offers a similar method of communication. It's almost like being there in person. Just don't try to make out with the screen.

GET FEARLESS

- Use Skype to connect when you cannot see each other in person.
- Never lick a computer monitor (or your cell phone).

FACEBOOK/TWITTER

Ahhhh, social media. Such a mixed blessing you have given us. On one hand, we are able to stay in touch with relatives and friends from around the world, regardless of how far apart our lives have taken us. On the other hand, those relatives and friends can see our every move and interpret them as they see fit. Our online digital footprints will always walk into our dating lives.

Facebook is an amazing the 21st century phenomenon. Never before have people been so willing to expose so much of our private personal lives. Revealing our whereabouts, sharing intimate pictures, and talking about what we ate for breakfast has become commonplace (for better or worse). Remember when people were freaking out about the advisability of using their credit cards to shop online? Facebook demonstrates that we have almost completely eradicated our concerns about privacy. But you still should be concerned. Your Facebook profile provides a ton of information—about you, your family and your friends. So when you're

Flirting Tip #29

Facebook can be a great way to stay in touch with people you care about, but think twice before you "friend."

flirting and looking to connect with people, that Facebook connection might need to wait a bit.

You said *what?* Misinterpretation and Facebook

In addition to pure privacy concerns, misinterpretation and runaway imaginations are two of the greatest dating pitfalls when dealing with Facebook. There is much that can be misread by people you're dating if they are your Facebook friends. People will read into things, people will take things the wrong way, or people will think that you are talking about them with every vague quotation you post.

It is to be expected that any new guy or girl you are dating that has made it into your "Facebook friend zone" will check out your Facebook page in great detail. They will look at your friends, read your posts, and go through your photos. Humans by nature are curious voyeurs. Their interpretations will have no real historical (or other) context, though, and may lead to some awkward conversations. I have personally witnessed many situations in which people who were casually dating friended each other and within a short period of time that relationship blew up because of what they found on each other's Facebook pages. Are you a girl who has a bunch of guys posting on your wall about how sexy you are? That might be a problem for your new boyfriend. Similarly, if you are a guy and your female friends are all over your wall telling you how much they love you and "thanks for last night," your new girlfriend of two months is probably going to get a little concerned. It might mean absolutely nothing, but the appearance of impropriety is all that is needed to start something unpleasant brewing.

Even worse are the people who friend *everyone* on Facebook. This includes *all* of the people they are dating, even when they are dating more than one of them at the same time. Can you imagine how messy that can get? Who needs that drama? So keep it simple and keep it to people you actually want to invite in your life. I'd suggest waiting to friend until you figure out if this new "friend" is going to be around beyond than the next holiday.

Flirting and Facebook

So now that I have scared you to even talk to your platonic friends on Facebook, let's talk about flirting! Flirting on Facebook can be fun, but you have to remember that it is not very personal. Unless you are sending private messages, everything you say to your crush is out there for all of your friends—and theirs—to see. I suggest keeping Facebook flirting limited unless you are in a serious relationship. Ways to casually flirt on Facebook include liking pictures, commenting on posts (within reason—it is easy to overdo it), and keeping your comments short and positive. You can also meet people through Facebook! See someone cute posting on a friend's page? Ask for an introduction if they are single. Using Facebook appropriately for the social network that it is can absolutely add some spice to your flirting—just keep it all in perspective.

Twitter and Flirting—Twirting?

As another huge social network that requires discussion is Twitter. People do in fact flirt on Twitter, but this is almost an entirely public platform. Moreover, Twitter is a space that is considered an indispensable marketing tool by many companies and brands—which means it is a very good chance that the people in your professional circle may view your conversations on Twitter. You can protect your tweets so only certain people see them, but it really isn't in line with the Twitter model, and most people leave everything out where the whole world can see it. Twitter is meant for people to interact in a very public way. So remember that when you are flirting on Twitter, you have an audience far beyond the object of your affection.

GET FEARLESS

- Think before you friend—give the budding flirtation some time to make sure this is someone you plan on keeping around and want to let into your life.

- Use Facebook to connect with friends of friends you find attractive—it never hurts to ask!

- Twirt with caution—everyone is looking!

11

Taking Over the World

*"Charisma is a sparkle in people that money can't buy.
It's an invisible energy with visible effects."*
- Marianne Williamson

Remember how at the outset of this book I said that flirtation is not always about sexual seduction? Well, that's the honest truth. Flirtation can be used every aspect of your life to make you more successful, make more friends, and simply connect better with people that you meet in any and every situation. I flirt nonstop. With everyone. I'm not just talking about people I want to become romantically involved with, but I'm also talking about people I want to connect with either professionally or platonically. For me, flirtation has always been about making other people feel good and boosting their confidence. When that is done in a platonic setting, you will still achieve the same result of someone being more inclined to like you, even if you don't want them to *like* you.

FLIRTING YOUR WAY TO SUCCESS

Flirting in business is an underutilized way to increase your success all around. Do you want to better connect with your clients or customers? Do you want to sell more? Do you want your presentations to have a greater impact? If the answer is YES, flirting can be the solution you need to achieve those goals. Ask any sales person if they flirt, and they will readily admit that they do. A good flirt can make an amazing salesperson (and vice versa). Not because they are trying to seduce you, but they are trying to make you feel comfortable and connected to them. So connected, that you will buy whatever they're selling.

If you are looking to get ahead in whatever you do, a little flirtation can go a long way. Your flirtations will be delivered in a slightly different version than the five steps described in chapter 5, but the foundation is exactly the same. The difference is *subtlety*. Your flirting prowess needs to be reduced a bit—tempered, if you will. Less is more, especially when it comes to interoffice communicating. For one thing, sexual harassment in the workplace is a valid legal concern, and never ever should your flirtations be able to be construed as seductive by an unwelcoming recipient. Obviously, there are office romances that arise out of the more "traditional" thoughts about flirtation—but right now we are focusing on purely professional relationships. When done correctly, there will be no doubt in anyone's mind that your flirting is purely platonic.

In business, flirting is all about using your charm and charisma to achieve results. Let's talk about the five steps when it comes flirting outside of the seduction:

1. **Eye contact**—Eye contact is always important, regardless of the particular conversation you're having. Even if you are not flirting at all, eye contact is essential to any connection. It shows someone that you are engaged and paying attention to what they're saying. In business eye contact can be even more important, since whether or not you maintain eye contact can be used to assess your trustworthiness. Shifty eyes or failure to connect have no place in a conversation where you are looking to win someone over.

2. **Smile**—You may think that a smile doesn't have a place professionally, but it definitely does. People want to work with people who are upbeat, warm and happy. It is that contagious positivity coming through again. There are certain times where a smile is inappropriate during business (e.g., a meeting about layoffs, discussion of legal

issues, etc.) and it will be up to you to assess the situation. However, letting people know you are human and welcoming is a professional asset.

3. **Conversation**—The art of conversation in business is essential. There are many people in this world that are unable to carry on good conversations. Ones that make the people you are speaking with feel like the focus is entirely on them. In business, you need to speak knowledgeably about your subject matter, but you can also interject appropriate compliments and humor. These compliments won't be based on your business associate's appearance, but their skills or achievements. Regardless, the compliments will resonate. Your humor (again, only if you are funny—and only if they have a sense of humor themselves) can endear you to them.

4. **Touch**—You may think that touch does not belong at all in the workplace, and depending on the situation, I would agree. However, a touch in the shoulder will almost never be mistaken as seductive and can help get your point across. Touching not-seductively, like a pat on the shoulder, can send subconscious signals to the person you are speaking to that "this is important," or that you are "passionate about this topic." Used sparingly, touch can be extremely effective.

5. **Body language**—Your body language might not be saying that you're interested in someone sexually, but it should demonstrate that you're open and listening to what your colleague saying. You still need to be facing

them with your shoulder squared off and in a position that won't make them feel like you're being defensive. So keep your arms open, your head focused, and your body directed towards them so that your associate feels that direct connection on the mental level.

Whether you are looking to nail that interview, or deliver a spectacular presentation, using these flirting techniques can give you the advantage you need to knock it out of the park.

Remember, regardless of who you are interacting with or for what purpose, using flirtation to connect on a human level will

Flirting Tip #30

Never stop flirting. Being a flirt and using your charisma can enhance almost every aspect of your life!

propel you to an even stronger connection. Making someone feel good through flirting is an art, and that art can lead to far greener pastures than you believed possible.

GET FEARLESS

- Use a subdued version of the five tips to super flirt to connect professionally and platonically.
- Use eye contact, a smile, conversation, touch and body language to escalate your success.

12

The Quiz

"To be tested is good." - Gail Sheehy

1. **When I think about dating and flirting, I:**
   a. focus on how much I hate my ex.
   b. think no one will like me.
   c. think it is fun and exciting.

2. **When I see someone I am attracted to, I:**
   a. run like hell.
   b. stare them down with my lips sealed.
   c. smile and make eye contact.

3. **When I'm talking to someone I think is hot, if they seem interested I:**
   a. start complaining about my ex-spouse.
   b. talk about how concerned I am that my Xanax prescription ran out.
   c. ask them questions about their last trip.

4. **I'm on a solo business trip in a city I'm not familiar with, so I hit up the hotel bar and:**
   a. make out with everyone in sight.
   b. get wasted on shots of tequila and eat the free peanuts.
   c. have one or two drinks and find someone to chat with.

5. **I got her number! I am going to:**
   a. call her incessantly. About every five minutes until she answers.
   b. leave creepy breathing noises on her voicemail. Because that's funny.
   c. call within the next three days and make plans to see her.

6. **I am getting dressed to go out, so I:**
   a. do a sniff test to see if my shirt is clean.
   b. find my favorite pair of hammer pants—the shiny ones.
   c. wear the outfit that makes me feel my sexiest.

7. **When picking a wingman, I:**
   a. don't pick just one! I travel in packs of 12!
   b. pick my least attractive friend so I look better by comparison.
   c. find a fun single friend who won't ditch me.

8. **I want to approach a woman I think is hot, so I:**
   a. tell her that she looks like she is high maintenance.
   b. stare at her until she asks me what my problem is.
   c. use something in the environment to start a conversation.

9. **I just had the best first date! I:**
   a. immediately take down my Match.com profile
   b. Google-stalk him, Facebook friend request him, and ask him if we can have "the talk."
   c. Go on another date tomorrow with someone else.

10. **Flirting is:**
   a. all about getting laid.
   b. all about manipulating people to do what you want them to.
   c. all about making people feel good, making yourself feel good, and making a connection.

Okay, let's see how you did:

Mostly A's:

Go read the book again. Pay serious attention to Chapter 4, because clearly you must have been drinking while reading to score this low.

Mostly B's:

See answer to "Mostly A's" and consider talking to someone. Professionally.

Mostly C's:

Give this book to a friend—you have got this! Stop wasting time on quizzes that you're on top of, and *get out there!*

CONCLUSION

As you can see, flirting is far from a science. It is an art form. Flirting is a way of communicating which will bring you stronger relationships, and better connections in every area of your life. Flirting is all about being genuine and authentic, and working towards making others happy.

Tapping into your inner flirt can help you meet people that you never would have been able to approach before, continue a conversation with them, and close the deal. I guarantee you that once you use these tips and practice, you will never be alone again (unless you choose to be). So when you are out in the world and going about your day, take a moment to use all of these skills in every area of your life. Be a little nicer to the person who pumps your gas, smile at someone on the subway who looks like they're having a bad day. All of these actions can bring so much more positivity to your life by bringing positivity to others.

Also, never forget to continue flirting throughout all of your romantic relationships. Flirting is important in keeping a romance alive. Continue to court each other and make each other feel good along the way. That's what it's all about. It's all about making people feel good. If you feel better in the process, it's a bonus.

Becoming a good flirt can eradicate all of the fears that you have ever had about meeting and connecting with people. Sometimes just flexing that muscle that has been dormant for so long can help to make you feel more confident, more outgoing, and all around more personable. I guarantee that if you have read this book and have implemented the things that we have talked about, you will make more meaningful connections. So go get your flirt on, and keep in touch—shoot me a note on www.theflirtexpert. com. I love a good success story.

ABOUT THE AUTHOR

Rachel DeAlto is a Flirting and Communications Expert who is dedicated to helping people communicate more effectively. Her expertise is available to help individuals who are single and looking for love, those trying to improve their current relationships, or any people who want to improve the way they communicate in any facets of their lives.

Rachel believes that "flirting" is an important skill in the vast toolkit of the art of communication. She believes that the art of the flirt is about giving compliments, making people feel good, feeling good about yourself, and spreading positivity. Rachel has always been in touch with her inner flirt. It started at birth when she wooed the nurses in the hospital to give her more attention, using her pouty lips and twinkling eyes. She further developed her communications expertise through her undergraduate studies which culminated in a degree in Advertising (which is really flirting with consumers) from the S.I. Newhouse School of Public Communications at Syracuse University, and later as a practicing trial attorney (a.k.a. flirting with the jury) after receiving her Juris Doctorate at Seton Hall University School of Law.

Rachel is also the founder and CEO of FlipMe flirt cards (www. flipme.com), which was developed to empower women to get in touch with their sassy confident side and make connections in the "real world" as opposed to online. Ever see someone in the subway who caught your eye? Or maybe in passing on the street, at a bar, in a café or pretty much anywhere? Weren't sure what to say or how to approach? FlipMe was created to make that connection a little easier, through the flip of a card. Each pack of FlipMe flirt cards includes 30 cards and a 6-month subscription to FlipMe. com. The cards contain flirty sayings on the front, and unique codes on the back that let the lucky recipient view your profile and send you messages on flipme.com. The packs come in Sweet, Sexy, Sassy or a Combo to let you match the sayings to your personality. Sweet cards saying anything from "Wink. Wink." to "Sometimes You Have To Take A Chance". Feeling sassy? Then you better be ready to hand out a card that says, "Here's Hoping You Can Read" or "I'm That Girl." The Sexy set is perfect for Vegas—where else can you get away with "Care to Be Mr. Right Now?" Never sure how you will feel? The Combo pack gives you one of each—30 different phrases for just as many moods and situations. It's simply a way to break the ice and let someone know you're interested in a fun way—without divulging your personal details.

Rachel has been featured on a multitude of media outlets including BetterTV, Cosmopolitan, Glamour, iVillage, The Nest, MSN, WPIX, LXTV New York, Cosmo Girl Sirius Radio, PlayBoy

Radio, Martha Stewart Sirius Radio, Yahoo Shine, and YourTango, and she is a featured expert with Howcast.com. For more information or to book Rachel for a media appearance or an event such as a workshop, seminar or keynote, please check out www.theflirtexpert.com.

CPSIA information can be obtained at www.ICGtesting.com
Printed in the USA
BVOW041547270213

314333BV00002B/98/P